Oldsmobile
A
War
Years
Pictorial

by Helen J. Earley and James R. Walkinshaw
1997

Credits

Photography
 All photos are from the Oldsmobile History Center except where noted. Negative sources include the Oldsmobile History Center and Leavenworth Photographics. Many thanks to Roger Boettcher for use of his vast file of negatives on Oldsmobile.

Dust Jacket and Cover
 Creative help from Jostens and Mike Lafferty, Okemos, MI

Printing
 Jostens

Copyright © 1997 by Earley Enterprises
 All rights reserved. This book may not be reproduced or quoted in whole or in part by any means whatsoever without written permission from:
 Earley Enterprises
 6200 Birch Row Dr.
 E. Lansing, MI 48823-1609

Manufactured in U.S.A.

ISBN: 0-9657968-0-9

Library of Congress Catalog Card Number 97-90353

Table of Contents

Introduction   4

Foreword by Robert J. Cook   5

Chapter 1
     World War I   6

Chapter 2
     World War II   12

Chapter 3
     The Korean War   168

Chapter 4
     The Years After   202

Appendix   206

Index   208

Authors Introduction

During the research for the Oldsmobile Centennial Book, "Setting the Pace," we found a wealth of photos and negatives which had never been used before. Many of those were used in that publication, including some from the war years. However, because of space limitations we were able to use only a few of the wartime photos which exist at the Oldmobile History Center.

In the past several years there has been considerable interest in the Second World War. We felt we should try to bring together as much of Oldsmobile's role during those trying years as well as other war related activities. This book is the outgrowth of that objective. We also thought we should try to complete it prior to Oldsmobile's 100th anniversary in 1997.

With that background we embarked upon another book. This time we felt that it would be best if we used as many of the photos as we could. For this reason, we decided to create a pictorial history of our war efforts. We have included over 500 photos and reproductions, some color and very little text except for photo identifying captions. The book covers Olds involvement in WWI, WWII, the Korean War and in later activities. Most of the photos are of the people, the plant and the various products we produced during these timeframes. The book is directed toward people who either worked at or had relatives who worked at Olds during these periods, or toward individuals who have an interest in wartime manufacturing or advertising.

We hope you enjoy your reading. We once again dedicate this book to the many Oldsmobile employes, past and present. For without you, this story would not exist.

Helen Earley and Jim Walkinshaw
August 1, 1997

Foreword by Robert J. Cook

When I started as a student at General Motors Institute in 1940, Oldsmobile was already getting involved in making war materials. When car production was suspended in early 1942, the plant was almost entirely engaged in making guns and shells. Most production was on a three-shift, seven days per week schedule. Building 40 was the "hub" of planning and tooling for the various plant projects. It housed the Plant Engineering, Plant Layout, Production Engineering Departments, Metallurgical Laboratory, Tool Room and Maintenance Machine Shops.

Helen and Jim have captured the photographs and essence of the war effort in this book. The activities in the plant were many and varied. The book brings back many memories.

Olds was always a family affair. We all worked together to produce large quantities of high quality war materials to support our Armed Forces.

The Korean war was a different story. This time, we were allowed to continue car production (at a controlled volume) and at the same time manufacture needed war materials. When the war ended, we were able to utilize the vacated space for a variety of automotive related activities. It helped us to reach the high volume car production of 1955 and beyond.

I'm sure you will find this book interesting and worthy of your time. It shows why we are so proud of our wartime efforts in support of our Armed Forces.

    Robert J. Cook, Retired
    Oldsmobile General Manager and
    Vice President General Motors

Chapter 1 World War I

World War I began June 28, 1914 and ended November 11, 1918. Oldsmobile's activities were limited to the latter part of the war. Car production was curtailed by the Government as demands for raw materials were met. Oldsmobile production was also affected by these restrictions. Olds' first contract was for 2,100 portable kitchen trailers for the aviation service. Announced on August 16, 1918, production began on September 1 and was completed by the first of the year 1919. No photos exist of the actual unit we made. The photo shown here is of a similar unit manufactured by another company.

Photo Courtesy Quartermaster Museum

World War I

In October 1918, the Oldsmobile Pacemaker printed this page. Olds was going to engage in further war work, the production of Liberty Aircraft Engines. Olds would cease car production for the duration of the War. Olds had been constructing a new engine plant (Bldg. 21) for the Northway V-8 engine. This would become the new Liberty Engine plant.

THE OLDSMOBILE PACEMAKER

Oldsmobile Plants To Be Entirely Devoted To Building Liberty Motors

The call has come to help win the war! And the builders of the Oldsmobile have chosen not merely to do their bit but to throw their every resource, every facility and every energy into the enormous task of backing up the men at the front. By the time this issue of the Pacemaker reaches our readers, the Oldsmobile factories will have become important cogs in Uncle Sam's mighty war machine "over here." In a matter of days passenger car production will have given way to Liberty Motors production. By the first of the coming year the project will be in full swing. And it will continue in increasing volume for the duration of the war.

Rush New Buildings

This important step is the result of plans begun months ago. When it became apparent that a considerable continuance of the war would require more and more help from America's steel manufacturing industries, the officials of the Olds Motor Works started shaping their affairs so that they might be of greatest possible service when the right time came.

Several months ago ground was broken for an immense addition to the Oldsmobile factories. Naturally many people thought this strange, were of the opinion that a postponement until after the war would have been more fitting. But the "handwriting on the wall" was plain. Should the nation require the Oldsmobile factories, this new building would surely prove a valuable adjunct. This surmise was correct. The new building plays a vital part in the Aircraft Production Board's program, and every possible means is being utilized to complete it in record time. In the meantime tentative plans for several other buildings that may be necessary are being drafted.

At the same time the task of recruiting the two thousand skilled workers that will be needed in addition to the present organization, is progressing steadily.

Every department of the huge plant is the scene of feverish activity. New machinery is being installed as rapidly as it is received. Factory executives and department heads are directing the many preparations necessary in order that the change to Liberty Motors production may be effected without friction or loss of time.

Passenger Car Production Halted

Very, very few if any more Oldsmobiles for civilian passenger use will be available until the Boche has been beaten into submission. So long as the war lasts, it is extremely probable that *all* our energies will be devoted to the making of war winning materials.

Of course this will mean disappointment to many, but we know that those who forego new cars will, like we, rejoice in making this additional personal sacrifice for the greatest cause civilization has ever known.

Service to be Maintained

Throughout the country Oldsmobile service is to be rigidly maintained however. Repair parts will be available. This is within the government's sanction and there seems no likelihood of any change in the attitude of the officials toward this important consideration.

Our thousands of friends may rest assured that nothing will be left undone that will tend to uphold the high standard of service so painstakingly established and jealously guarded throughout more than a score of years.

Au Revoir

Now that the force of circumstances makes advisable the temporary suspension of the Pacemaker we find it hard to express fully our deep appreciation of the fine spirit of helpfulness that has at all times been accorded it by the friends of the Oldsmobile.

We know that the Pacemaker has been the means of bringing us into intimate contact with thousands. This has resulted in mutual regard, in an understanding of each other's hopes and ambitions—in a word, in friendship.

Fortunately, this is not our farewell. The end of the war will find the Oldsmobile factories greatly enlarged and wonderfully equipped. Thousands of new workers will have been trained to the very acme of mechanical skill. All of these vast resources will be diverted to Oldsmobile building just as soon as the country's needs are satisfied. More Oldsmobiles than ever before will be built—better Oldsmobiles if that is possible.

So now we say *au revoir* in the hope that very soon the world catastrophe shall have been completely averted and we may meet again in the normal pursuit of happiness.

Pacemaker Suspended for Period of War

MUCH as we regret to disturb the pleasant relations that have been established by the Pacemaker between the members of the Oldsmobile organization and their almost countless friends, present conditions force us to the conclusion that it is no more than our patriotic duty to suspend its publication until peace returns.

The scarcity of print paper is becoming so acute that the government is strenuously urging extreme conservation. The labor involved in printing, binding and mailing each issue can well be diverted to more essential channels.

After the war we sincerely hope to at once resume publication; to pick up the threads where they have been severed; to re-establish this bond of friendship.

World War I

On October 1, 1918 Olds announced that they would be manufacturing Liberty Engines. The Liberty Aircraft Engine was a standard "V" designed engine that was being made by a variety of engine manufacturers. Amoung them was Buick which had been making the engine for some time. Olds was fortunate to have Building 21 under construction at the time. This center spread appeared in the Pacemaker on October 18, 1918. You will note several construction photos of Bldg. 21. The large group of people is in front of Bldg. 20 which was part of the Assembly Plant at that time. From the looks of the size of the group, it would appear that all the plant employes were standing there for the photo.

World War I

Right-This ad ran in the October 19, 1918 issue of *Automobile Topics*. Olds told the world that the War took priority over car production.

Below right-The Liberty Aircraft Engine. The engine had been designed for manufacture by a variety of companies. It also came in several configurations, this one being a V-12. The war ended rather abruptly with the signing of the Armistice on November 11, 1918. Olds never got into production and Bldg. 21 was used for manufacturing V-8 automobile engines instead.

Prior to the end of the war, Olds had been asked to bid on two other items for the war effort. In early October 1918, bids were submitted for the production of trousers to the Manufacturing Branch, Clothing and Equipage Division, Quartermaster Corps in New York. Ours was one of over 460 bids submitted for clothing, most from established clothing manufacturers.

In early November, contracts were placed with Olds for "engine spares" from the Bureau of Aircraft Production. It is unknown if this related to the Liberty Engine contract or if it was just for other engine parts. In any event, it is likely that all the contracts were cancelled prior to actual production since the war ended in the same timeframe.

Opposite page-The Economy Truck was designed in this same era. Production started shortly after the end of the war. A good many trucks were used during the war and some of them looked very similar to the Olds version. We may have designed this vehicle to be used in the War effort although no records indicate any were sold to the Government.

For Liberty, Democracy and the Duration of the War

Oldsmobile

efforts will be devoted solely to the service of the United States Government.

All the mechanical skill of our great organization, that for twenty-one years has kept Oldsmobile in the forefront of the industry, is now dedicated to Victory —in building Liberty Motors.

To the many thousands who know the Oldsmobile:

We know that you are behind us in this great undertaking.

And we simply say, When the War is Won, we shall be able, with our greatly enlarged plant and our increased facilities, to serve you better than ever before.

OLDS MOTOR WORKS
Lansing   Mich.

Photo Courtesy GMI Alumni Historical Collection

World War I

*Oldsmobile Economy Truck
The Lansing Station*

Chapter 2 World War II

The United States was engaged in WWII from Pearl Harbor on December 7, 1941 to VJ day on August 14, 1945. Oldsmobile's war effort started long before the United States entered the War. The Forge Plant (Plant 2) would be the first to start munitions production. GM had purchased the plant on May 22, 1940 to be used as a heavy press plant for producing automotive forgings. However, before the plant became operational, Olds submitted proposals for 75mm and 105mm shells on September 16, 1940. We were awarded the first contract on November 20, 1940. Plant 1 would enter war production when the 20mm cannon contract was awarded in April 1941. Car produc-

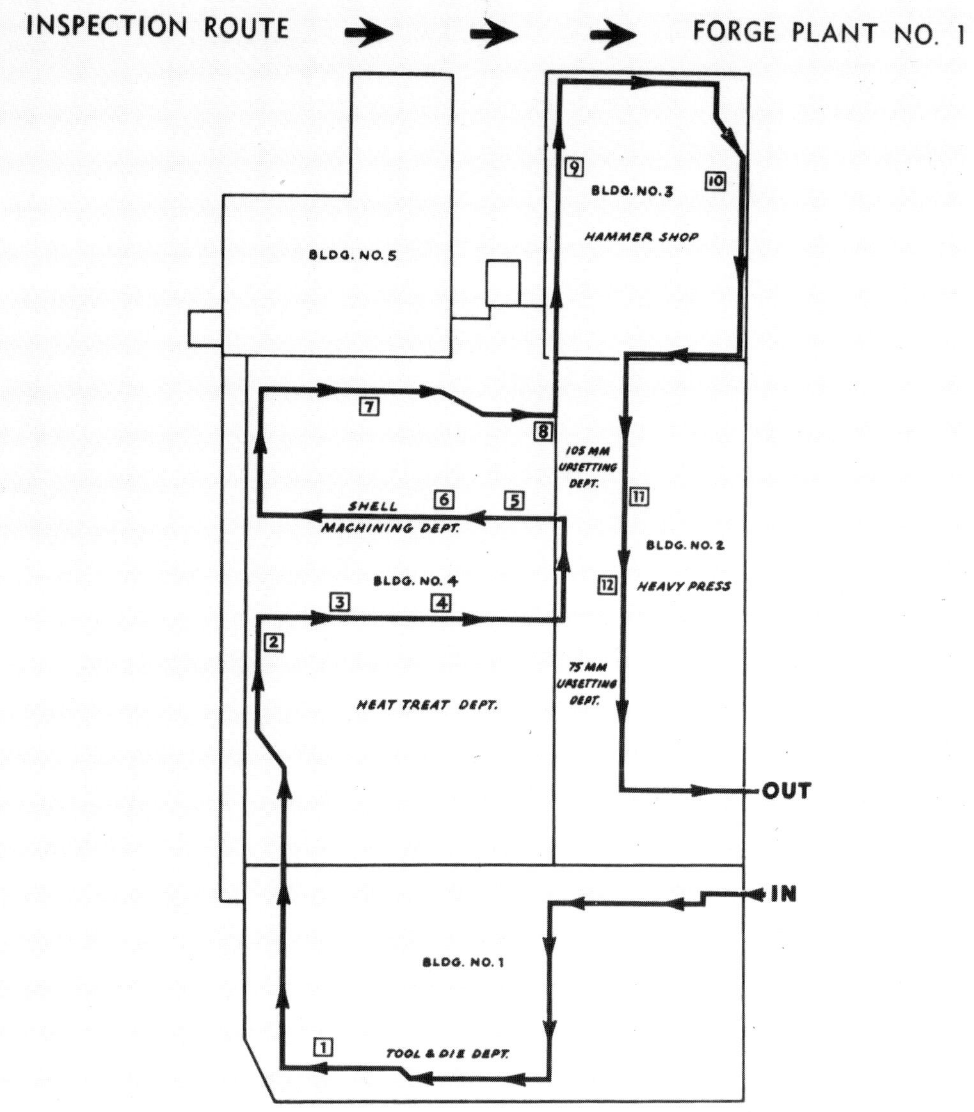

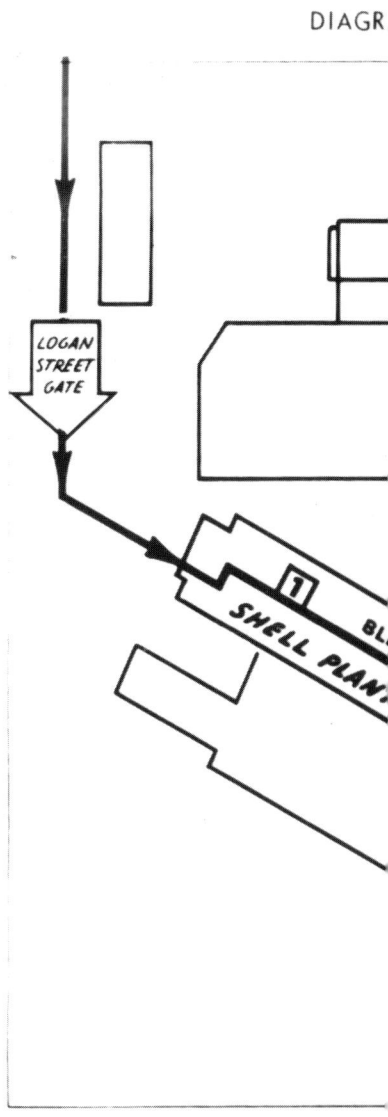

FOLLOW THE RED ARROWS

The route through Forge Plant No. 1 passes through the Tool and Die Department, the Heat Treating, Machining, Inspection and Painting Departments and then into the Hammer Shop, the Press Department and the Upsetting Department. First, you will see forging dies in the making — next, 75 mm. M-48 and 105 mm. M-1 High-Explosive shell in production — next, heavy forgings under hammer and press — and, finally, the upsetting process of forging shell bodies.

FOLLO

Passing first through Shell Plant you see in production Armor-Pierc Navy 3" MK 29 and the 75 mm plants where production operations M1A1 and 3" M7 tubes may be c

World War II

tion would not cease until February 5, 1942. From then on it was "Fire-Power is our business" until the war ended in 1945. The plant "Keep-'em-firing" committee made up of union and management people would push production and our commitment to Fire-Power. That is what Oldsmobile did for the duration!

The two maps shown here are from an open house held at the plant and published in a Fire-Power Booklet given out that day. Plant 2 is below left and Plant 1 is to the right. The tour routes are noted with numbers placed along the route. The description at the bottom defines the major activities in the plant in the early part of the war.

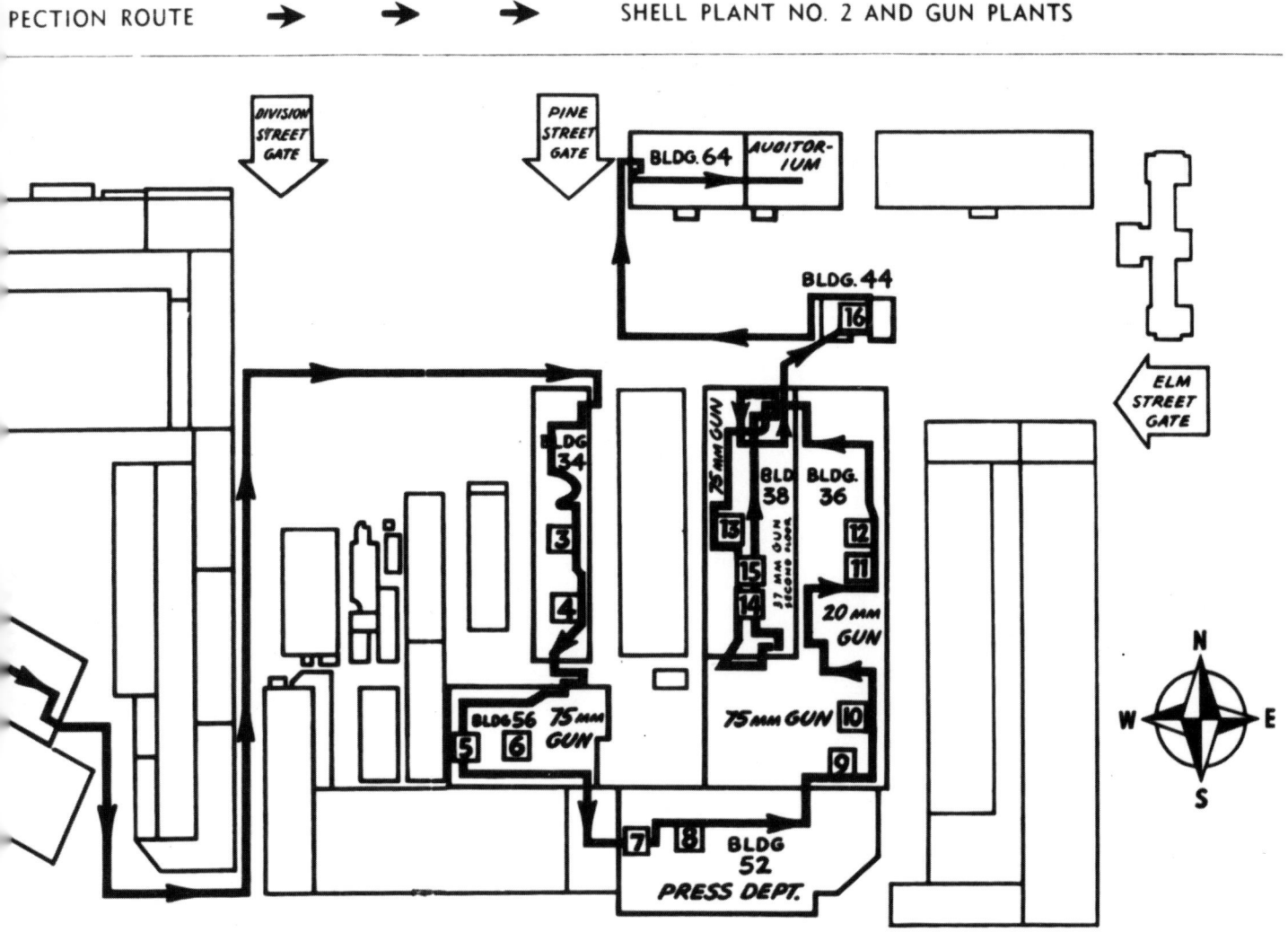

PECTION ROUTE → → →   SHELL PLANT NO. 2 AND GUN PLANTS

ARROWS →

d on Oldsmobile's main plant grounds. rojectiles of two different types — the the route takes you through the gun m. M3 Tank Cannon, and the 76 mm. follows inspection of important operations on the 20 mm. M2 and the 37 mm. M9 Automatic Aircraft Cannon. On each of the 75 mm., 76 mm., 20 mm. and 37 mm. guns, Oldsmobile builds the three most important parts — on the 37 mm. gun, a number of additional parts as well. Other parts are built by sub-contractors. All four guns are assembled by Oldsmobile and two of them — the 20 mm. and 37 mm. Cannon — are test-fired in Oldsmobile's proof range.

Note: The route through Oldsmobile's 37 mm. gun plant, which is on the second floor of Building 38, is indicated above by black arrows rather than red.

World War II

Guns

The **large photo** shows the construction of the 20mm M2 cannon produced from October 16, 1941 to January 31, 1944. Olds made only three parts for this gun, the barrel, receiver body and bolt. The rest were purchased from outside suppliers. This gun weighed 113 pounds and fired a 0.29 pound projectile. It was used in a great variety of aircraft.
Below-20mm cannon with feeder.
Below center and bottom-Gun machining operations.

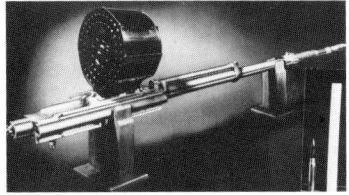

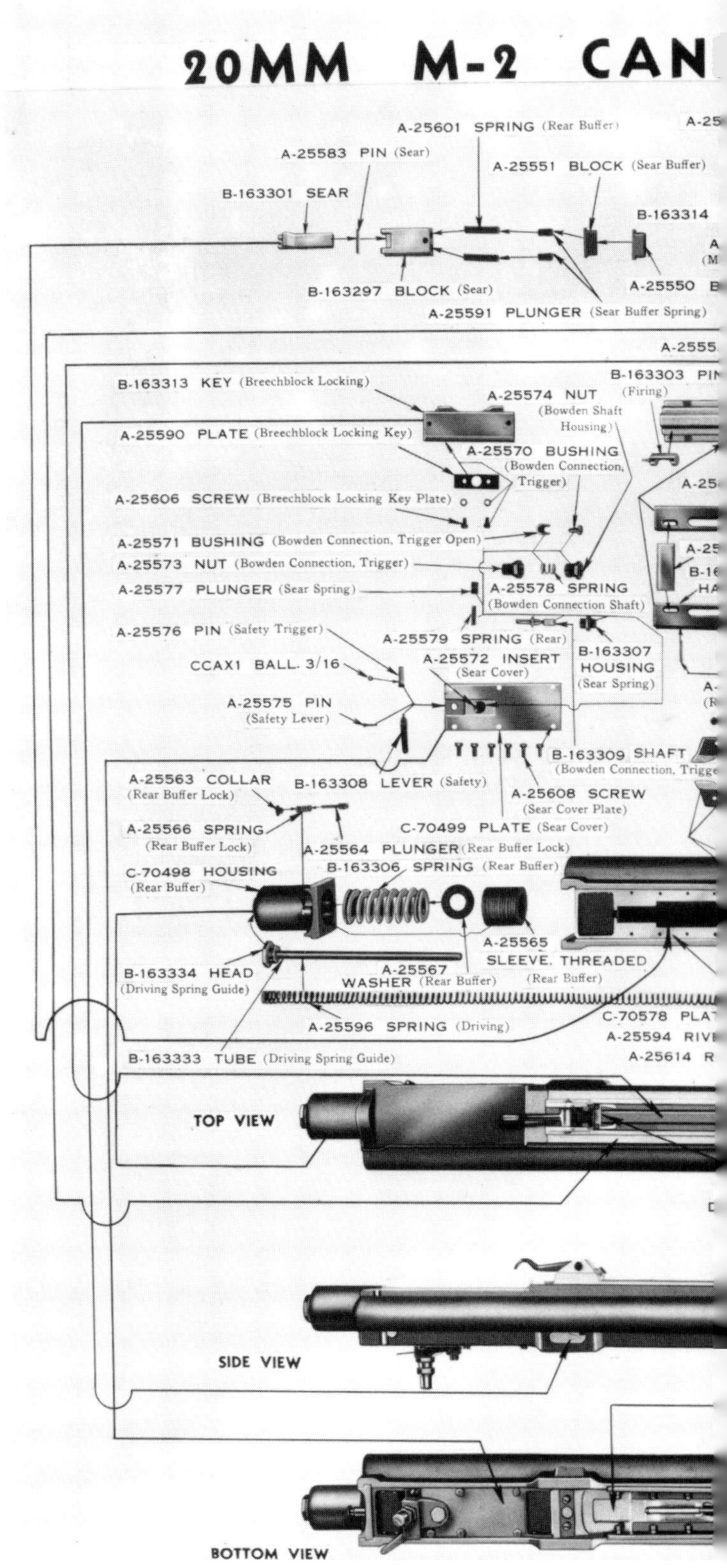

World War II
Olds Motor Works Gun Division

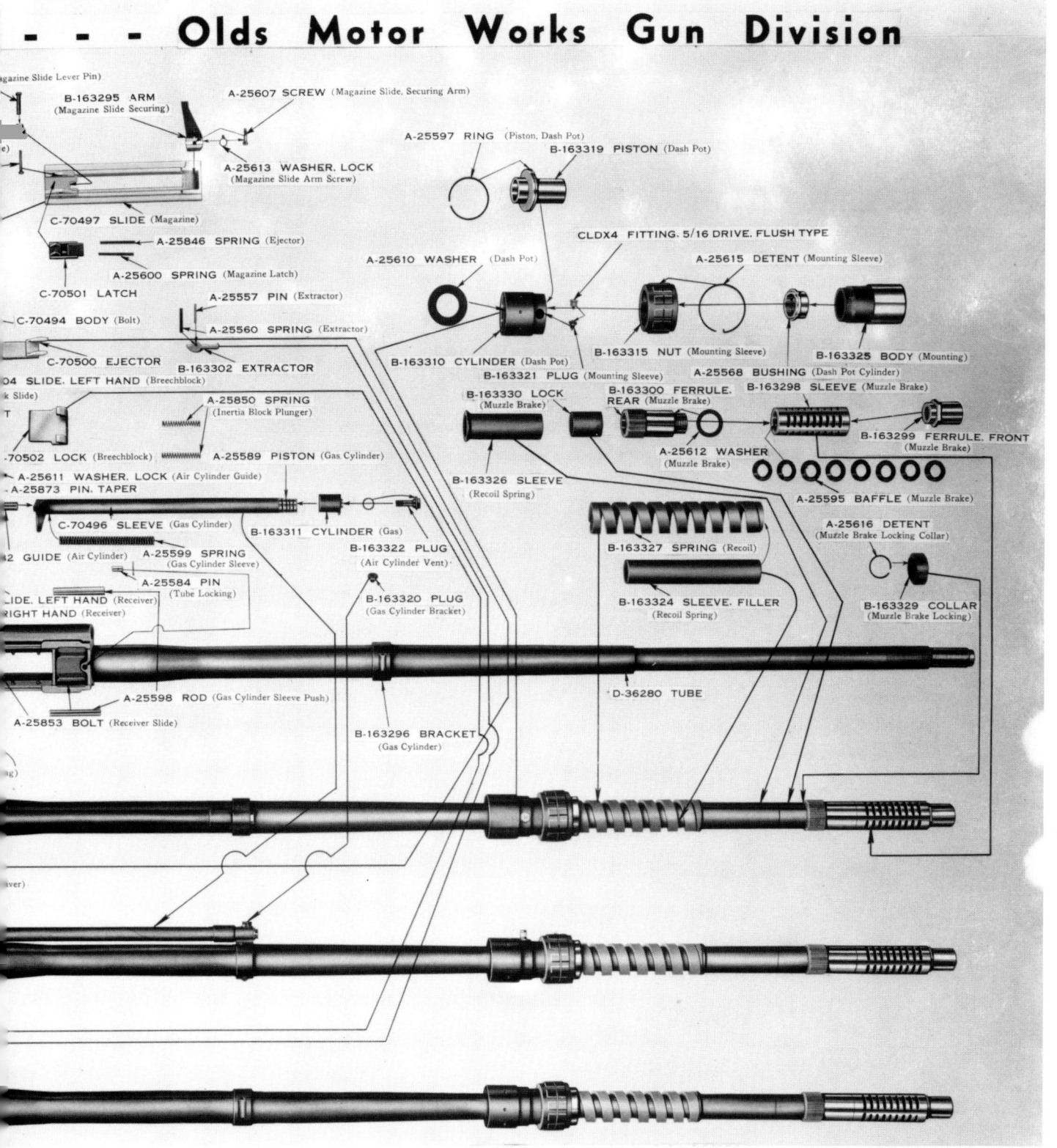

World War II

Guns

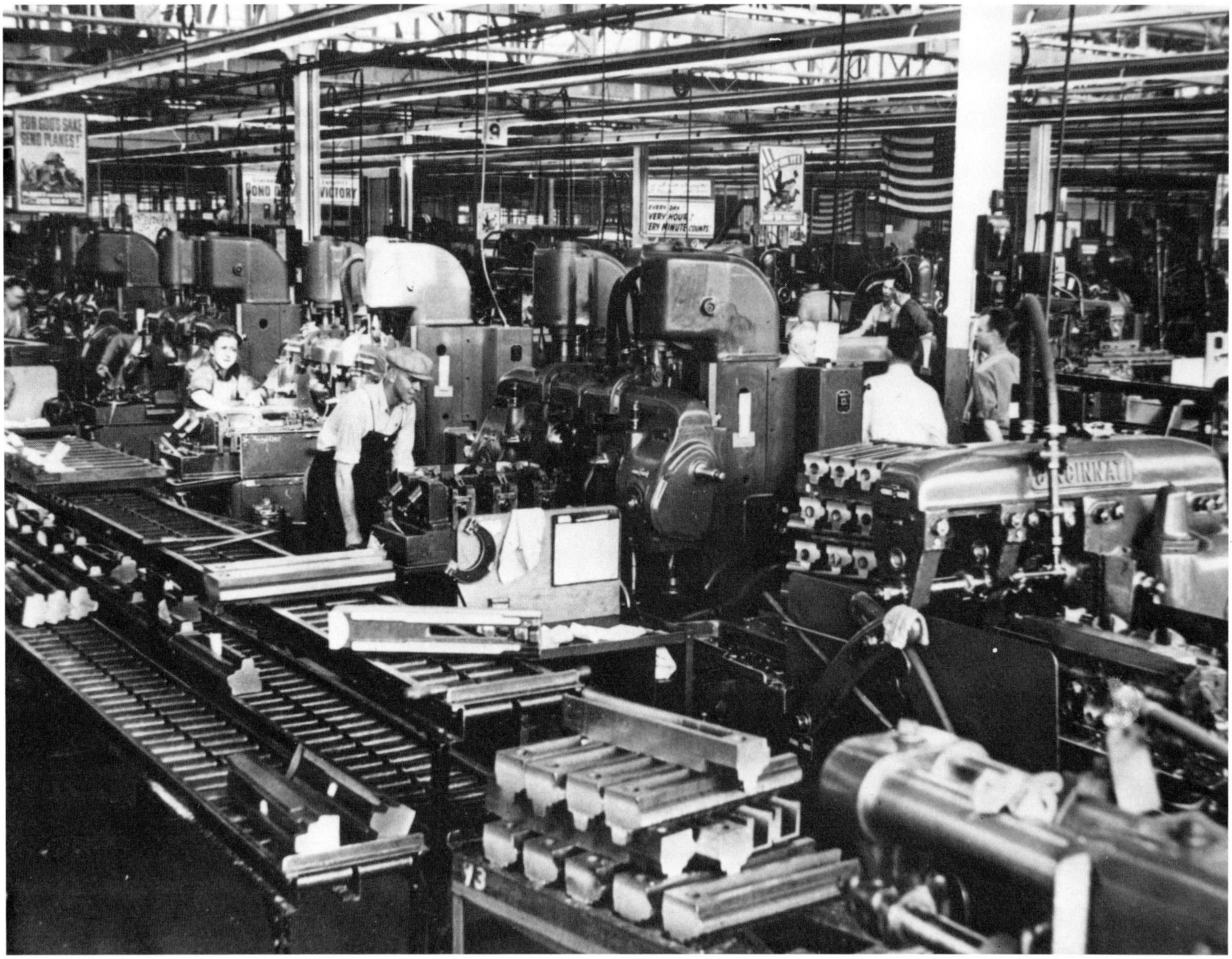

World War II

Guns

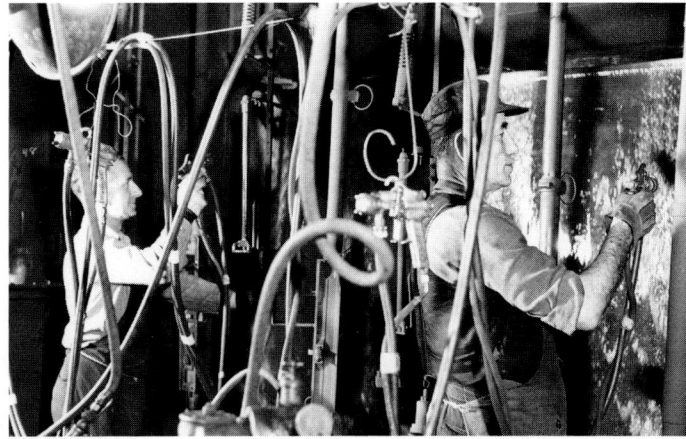

Opposite page top-Machining the receiver body. This part was machined all over. You will note the use of tool room milling machines on many of the operations. **Bottom**-Assembly in Bldg. 36.

This page top left-Gun tube rifling area. **Top right**-Tube painting. **Left**-Loading boxed guns into railroad cars. **Bottom**-Gun displays made by Exhibit & Display.

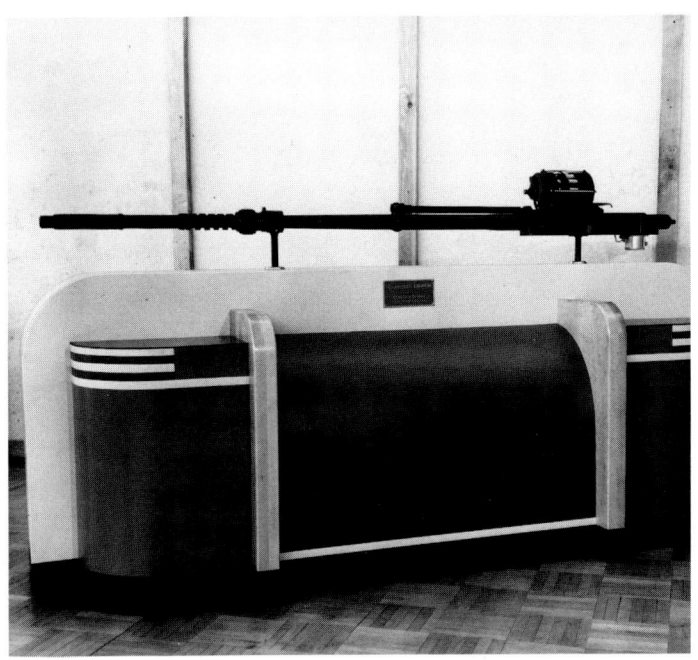

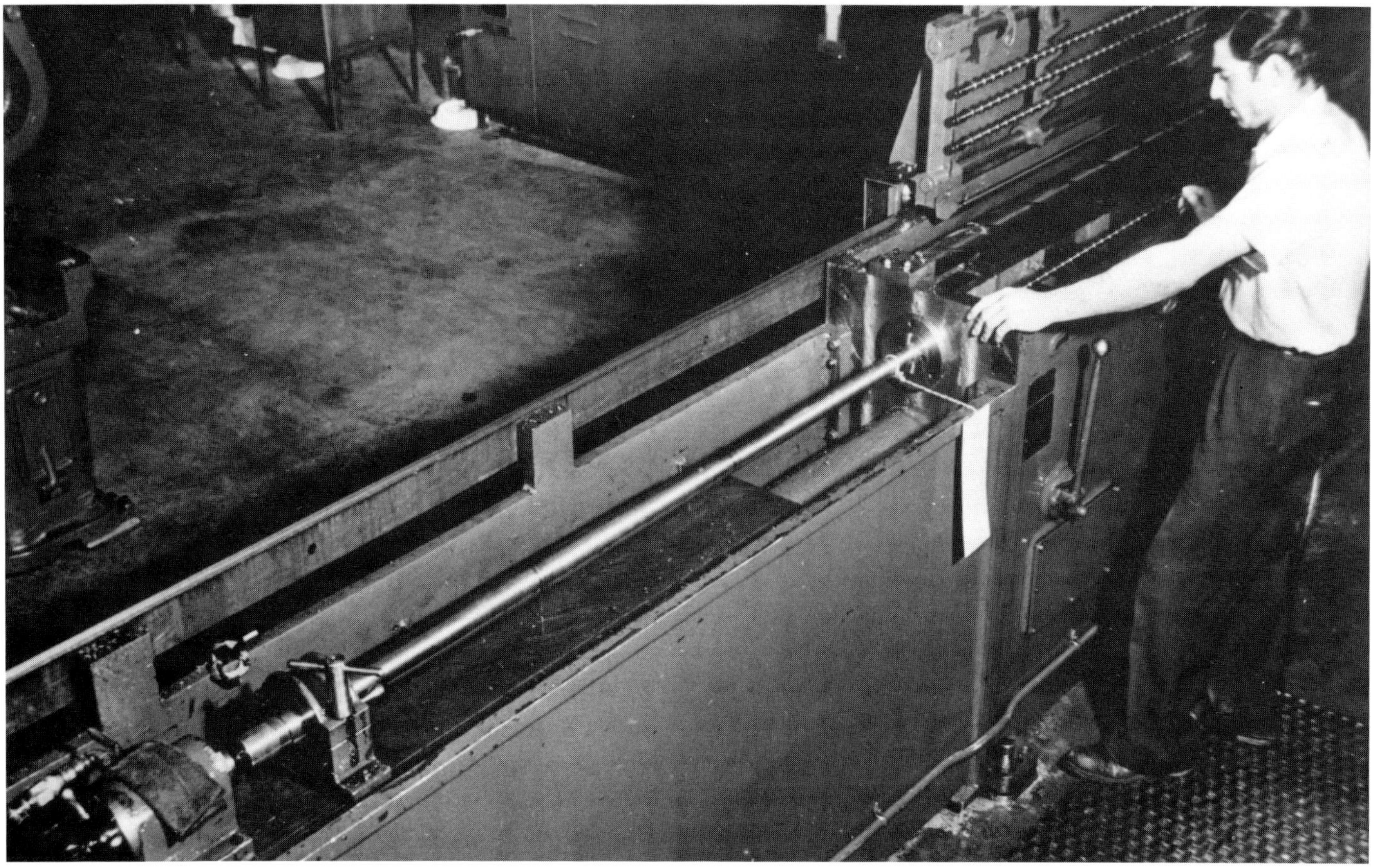

World War II

Guns

18

World War II

Guns

Oldsmobile did considerable work on improving the manufacturing process for the various guns it produced. These activities allowed us to reduce the cost and selling price over the life of the contracts. Barrel rifling is typical of these.
Opposite page top-Pratt and Whitney manufacturing used the typical single tool method of doing this task two barrels at a time at about the rate of one barrel per hour. **Opposite page bottom**-Olds developed a new method using an American Broach machine for broaching the rifling at the rate of six barrels per hour.
This page-Chart below indicates the improvements made in a variety of other parts. Barrel life was normally 5,000 rounds. Our goal was to improve each major component to this level to reduce field maintenance. You will note in all but three cases we were able to exceed this goal.

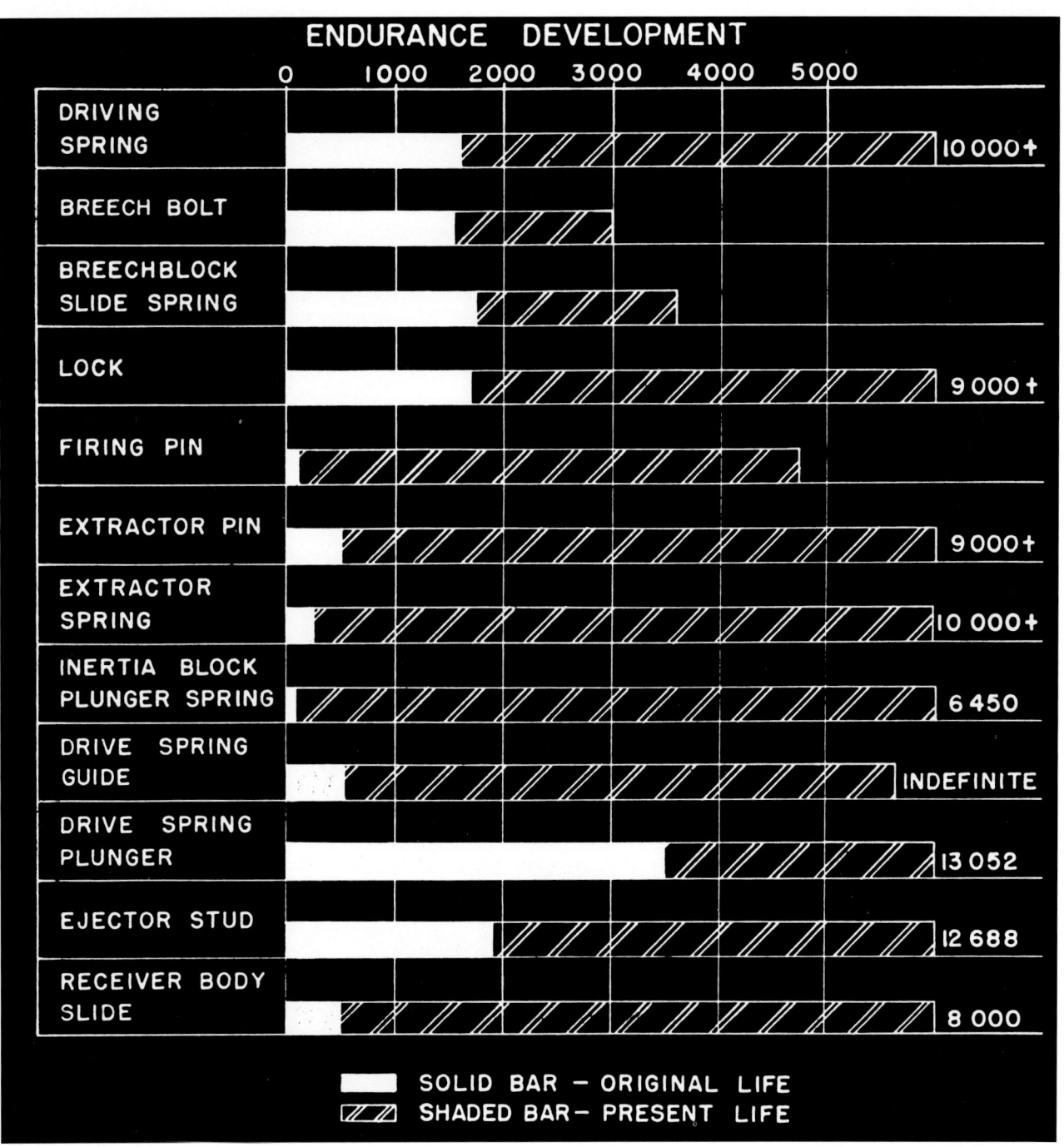

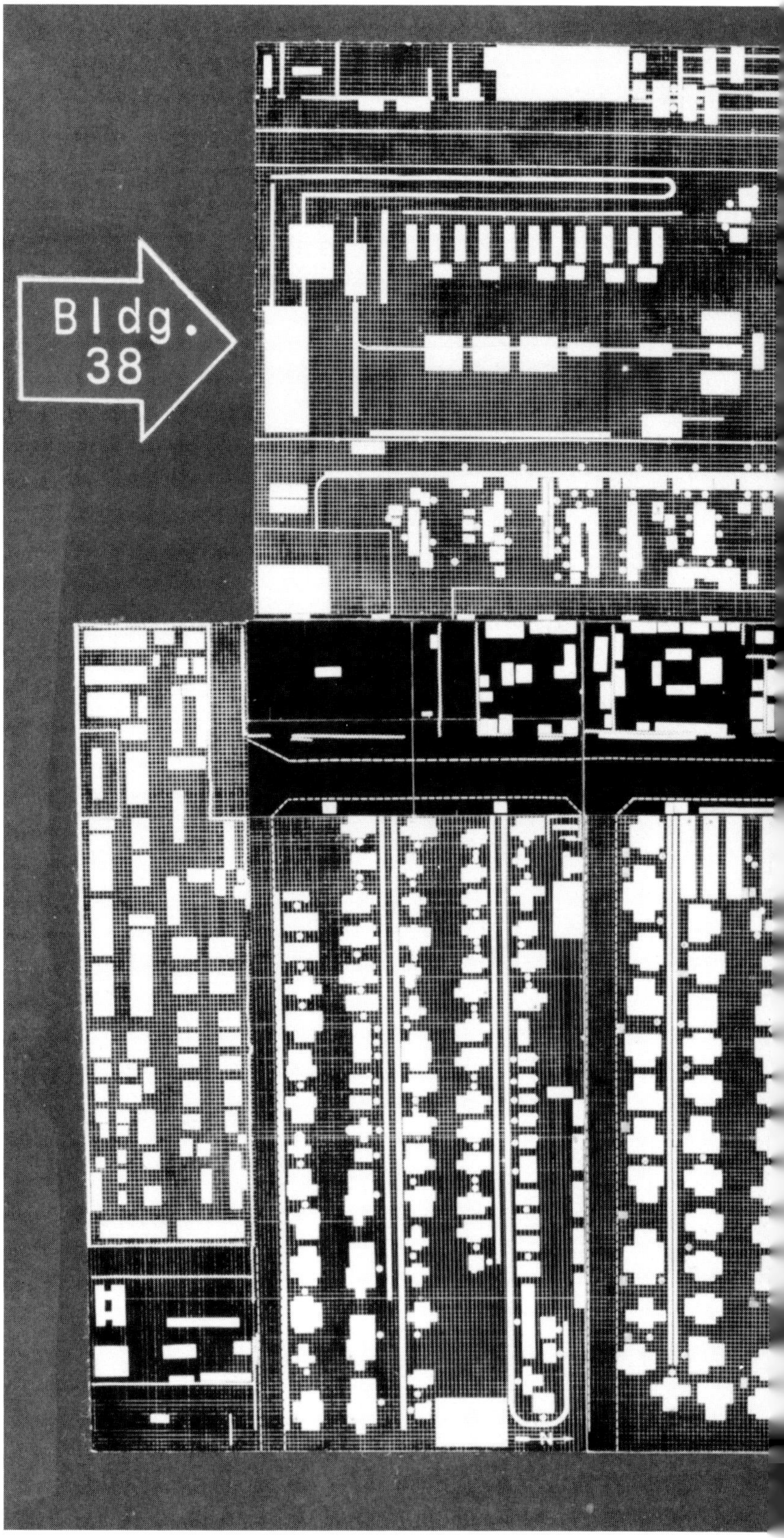

Guns

World War II

The 20mm production floor as it was on the Plant Layout two dimensional layout. Most of the activites were in Bldg. 36.

20

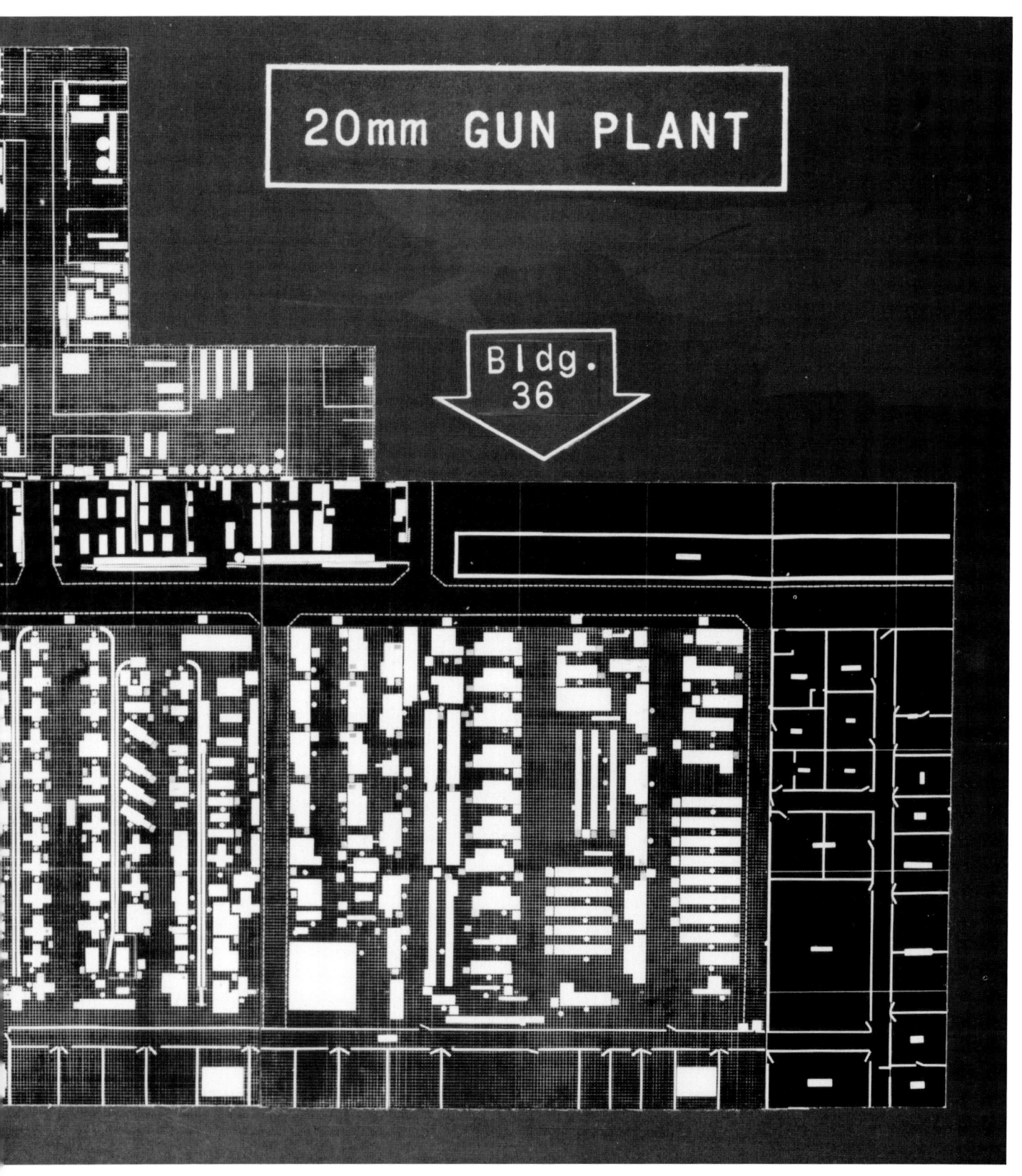

World War II

Guns

37mm M4 gun layout. Olds produced this gun from July 12, 1942 to June 16, 1943 making 2,779 of these aircraft service guns. The gun weighed 216 pounds and fired a projectile weighing 1.66 pounds for armor-piercing applications or 1.34 pounds in the high-explosive variety. The gun was produced in Bldg. 38 on the second floor.

Below-The 37mm M4 gun.
Bottom-The 37mm M1A2 anti-aircraft version. Only 150 of these were made.

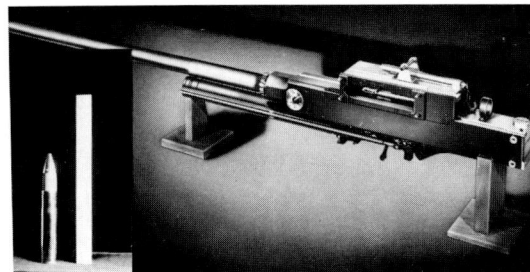

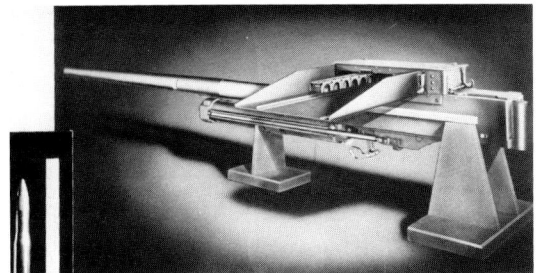

World War II

Guns

OLDSMOBILE GUN DIVISION

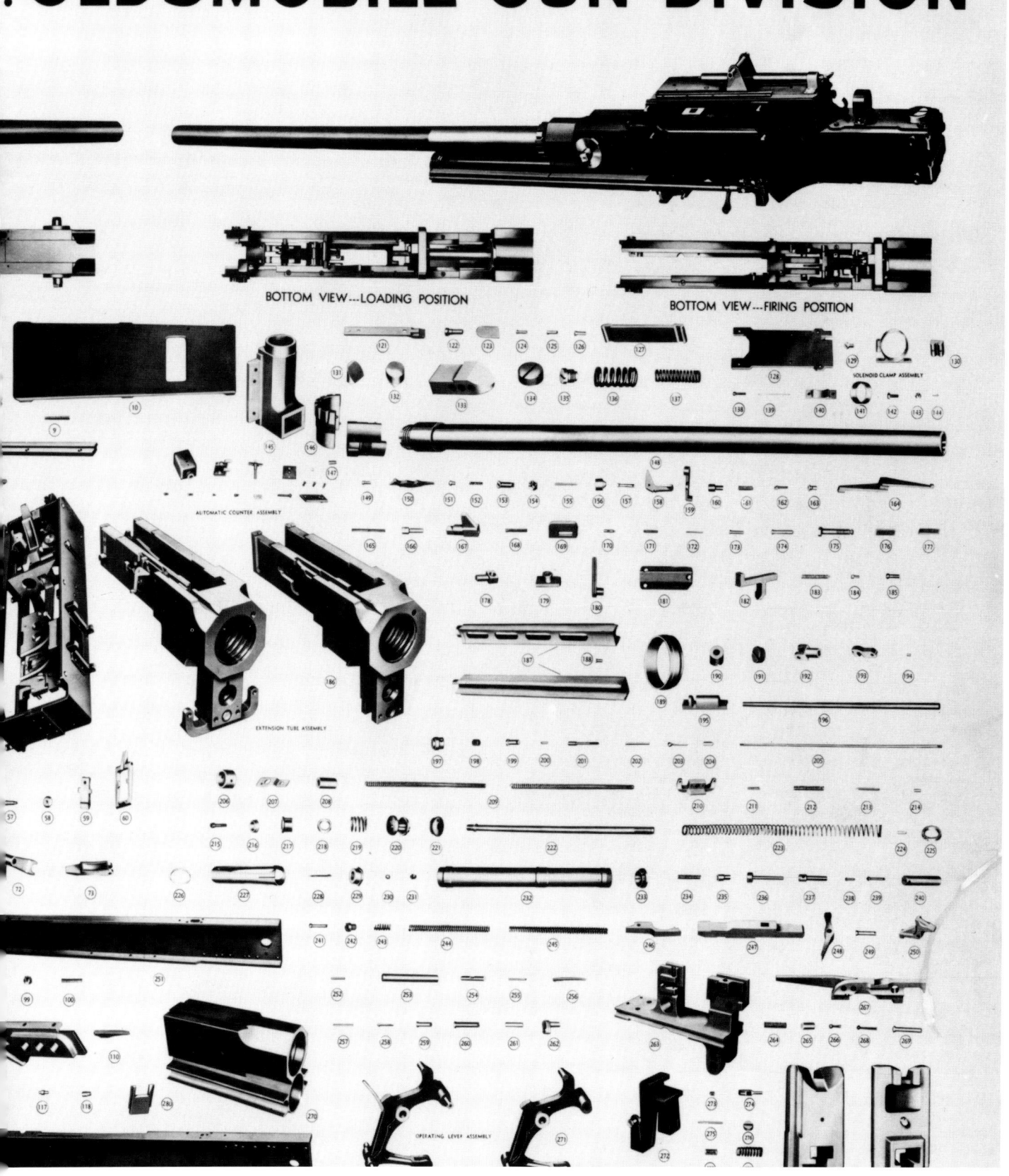

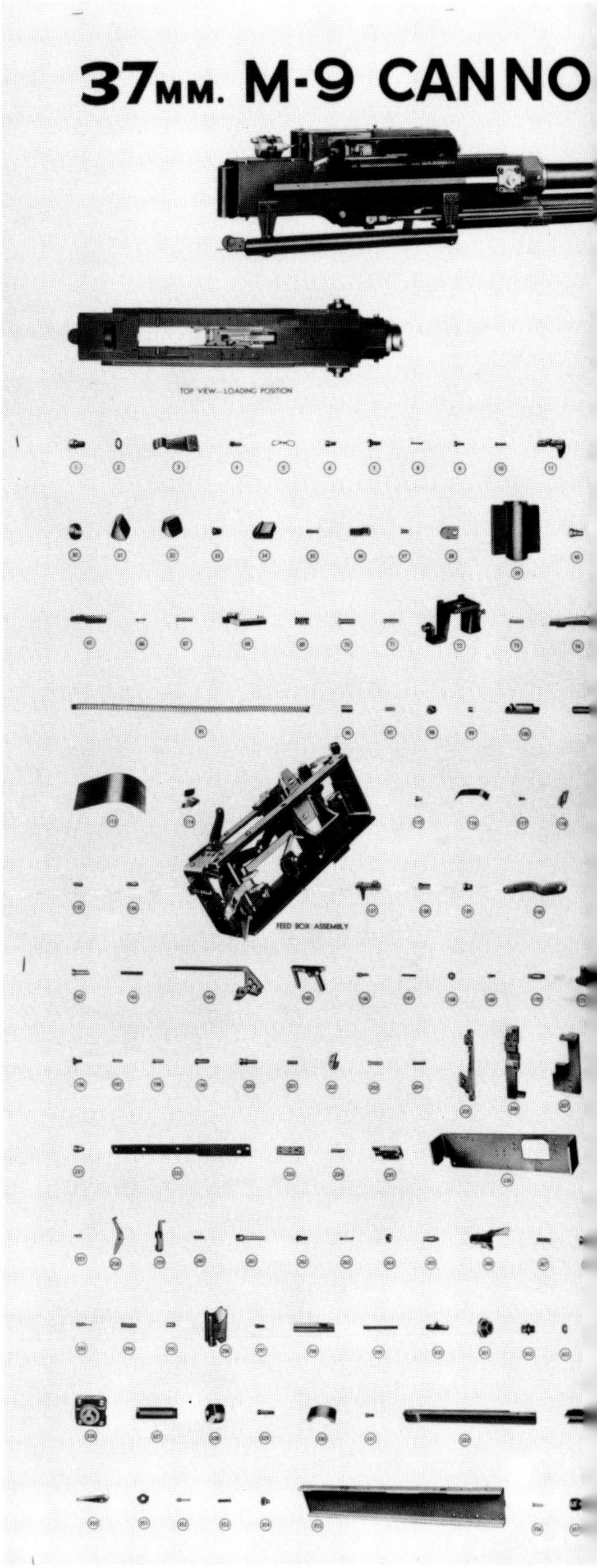

World War II

Guns

37mm M9 gun layout. Olds produced this gun from May 23, 1943 to May 16, 1944. 2,930 of this type of gun were made. **Below**-M-1A2 37mm anti-aircraft cannon.

World War II

Guns

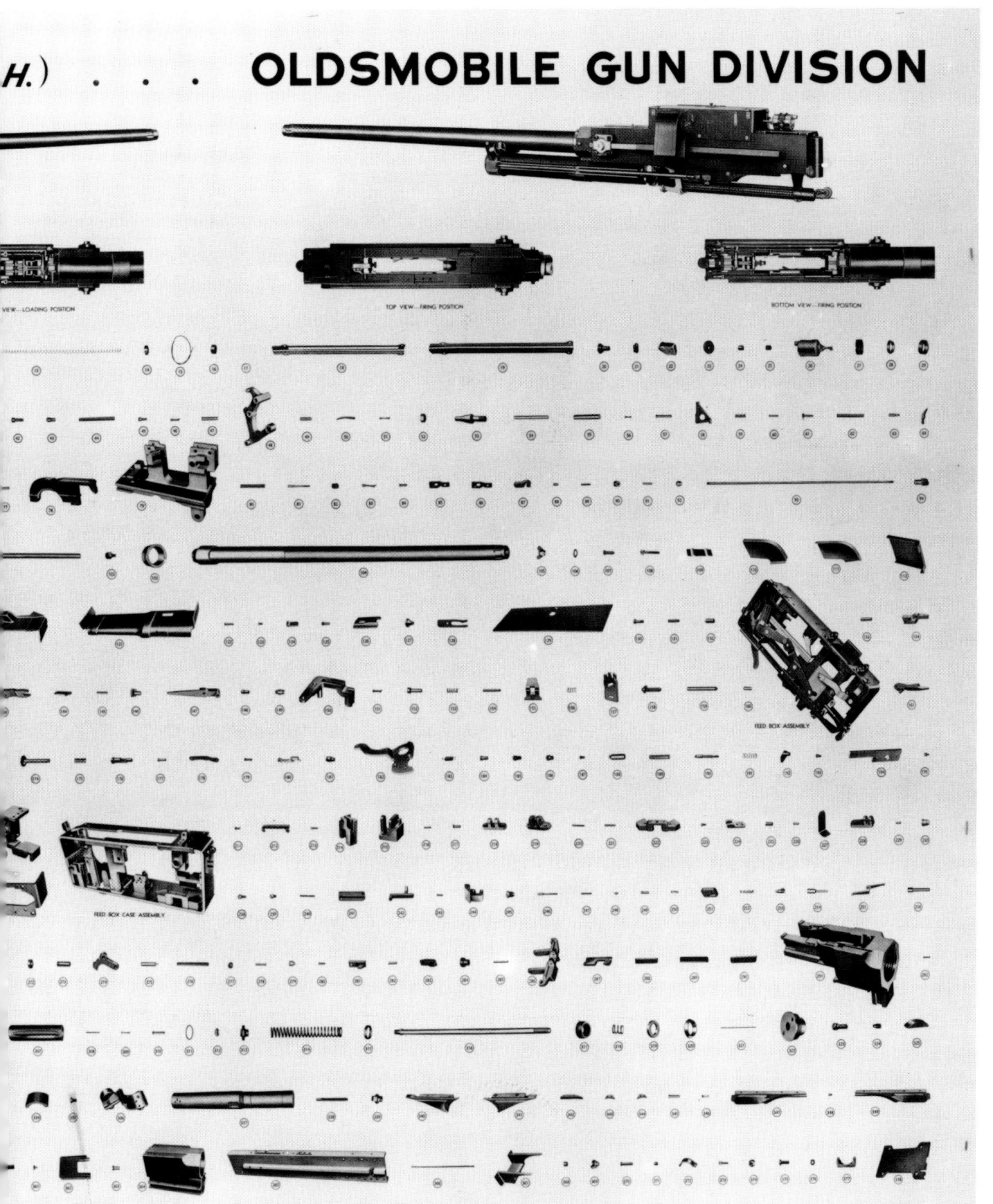

World War II

Guns

This page below-37mm gun area. Operation appears to be a repair or tear down area since there are several completed guns on the floor behind the two men. **Bottom left**-A 37mm gun display. These displays were made by the Exhibit and Display Dept. in Bldg. 64. The display is photographed at that location. **Bottom right**-Gun boxing.

Opposite page-Other gun displays. Many displays were for the public.

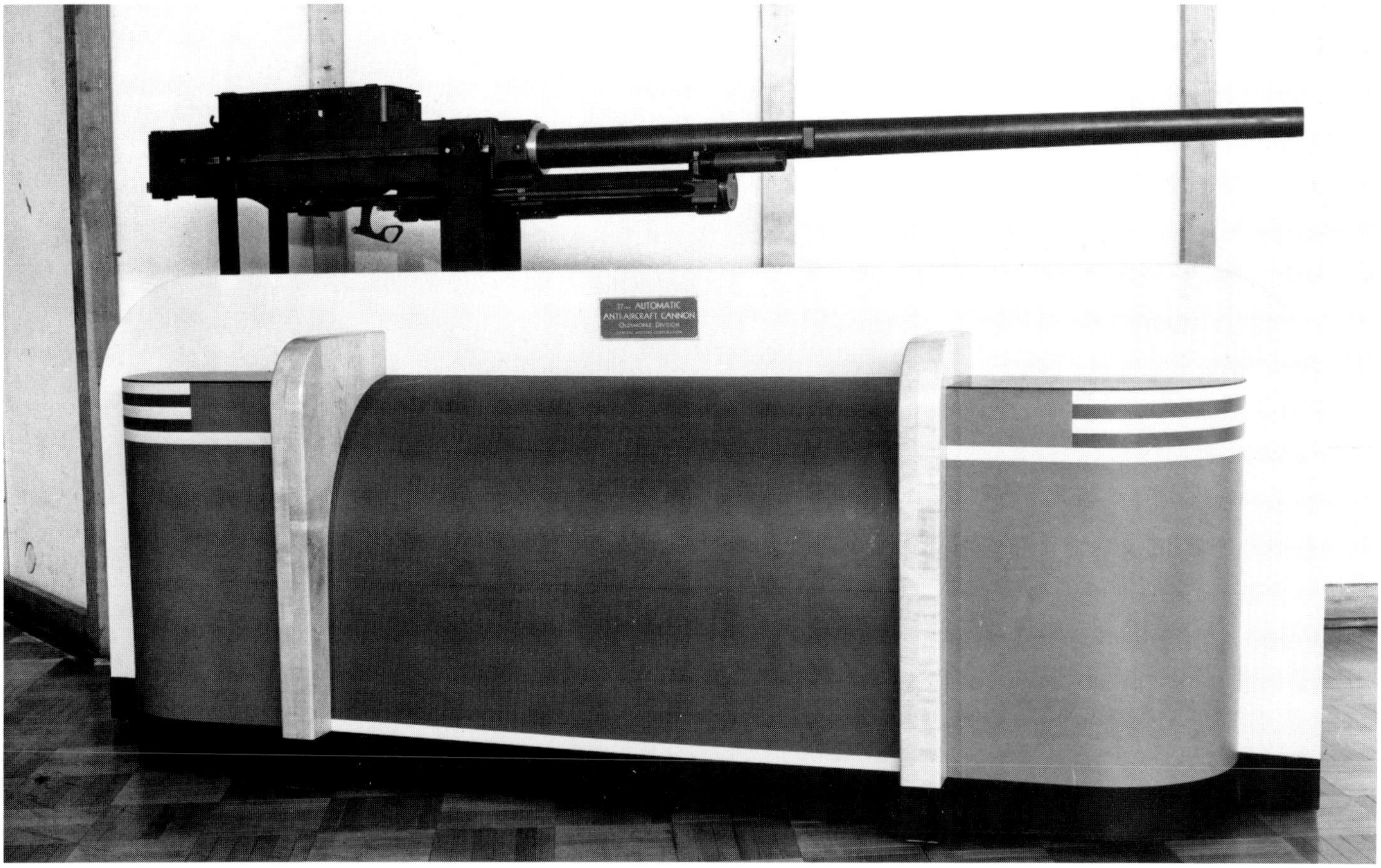

World War II

Guns

World War II

Guns

Right-37mm M-1A2 cannon display. **Below**-Building 38 second floor 37mm cannon floor layout.

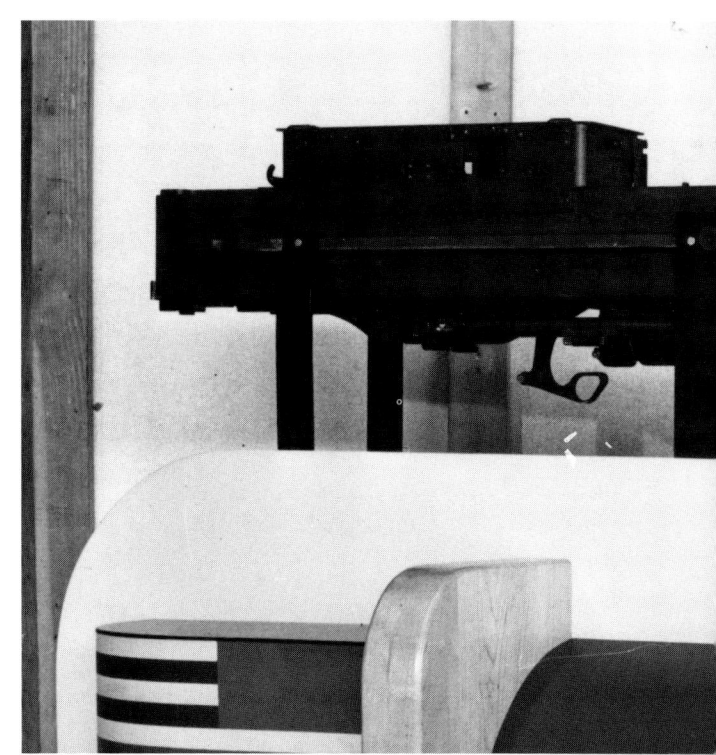

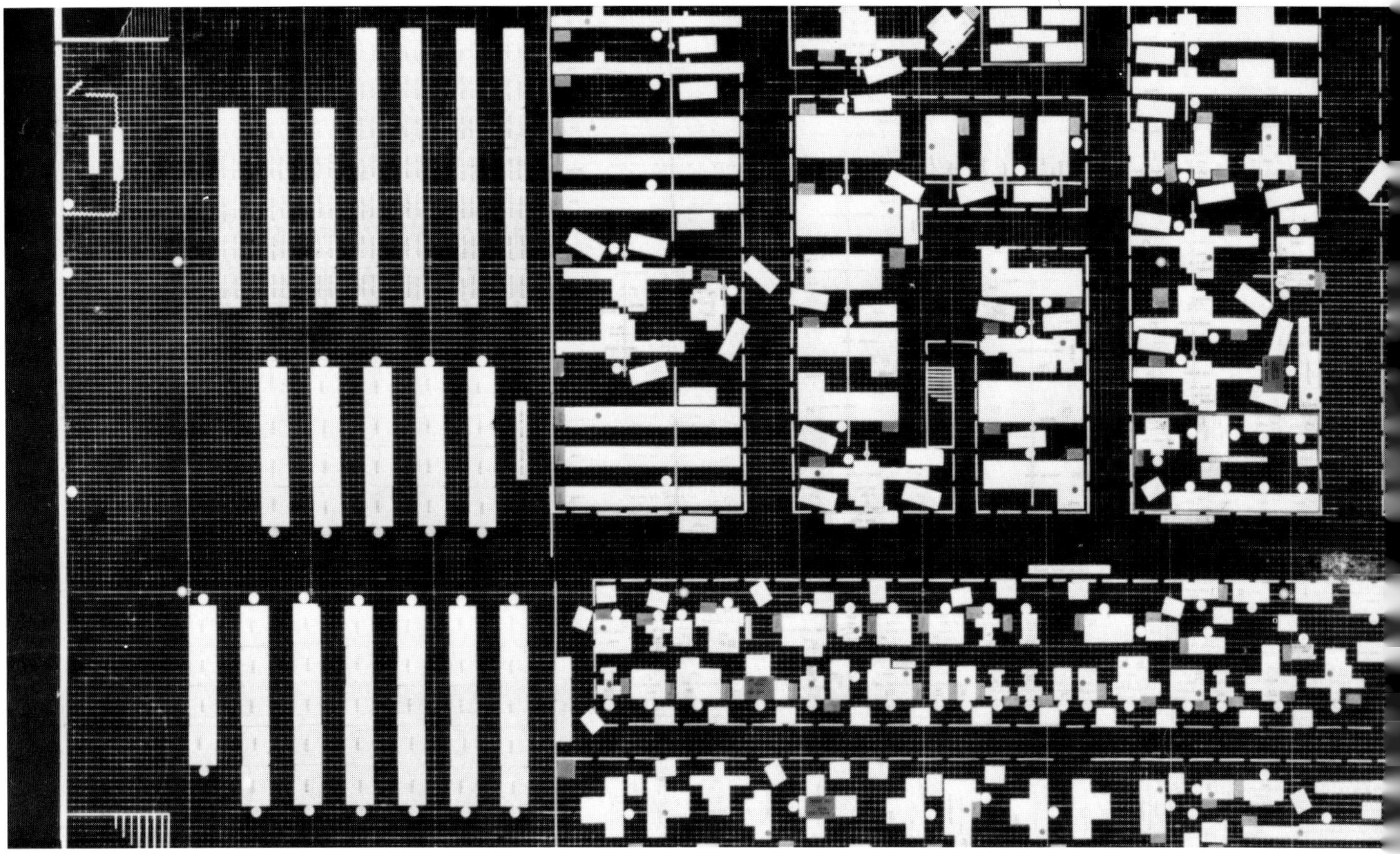

World War II

Guns

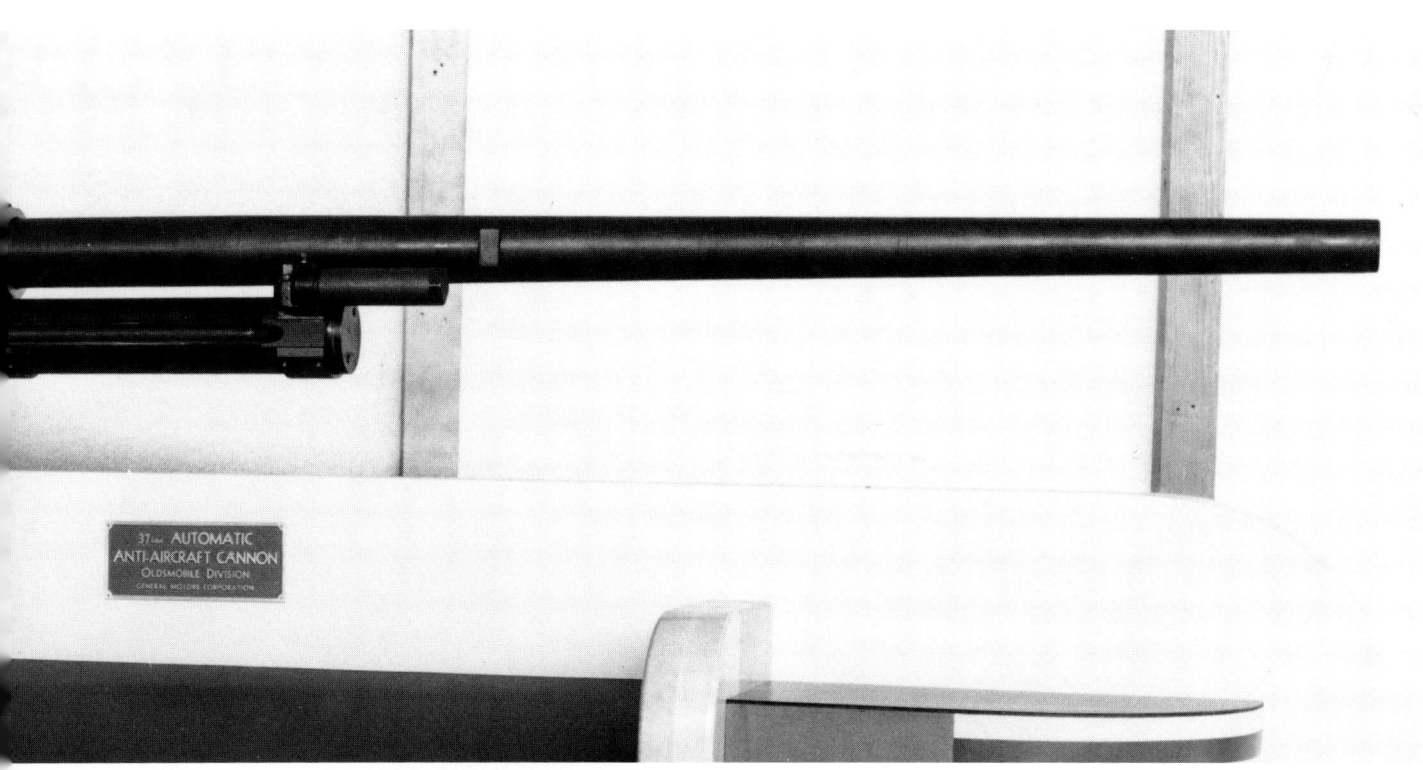

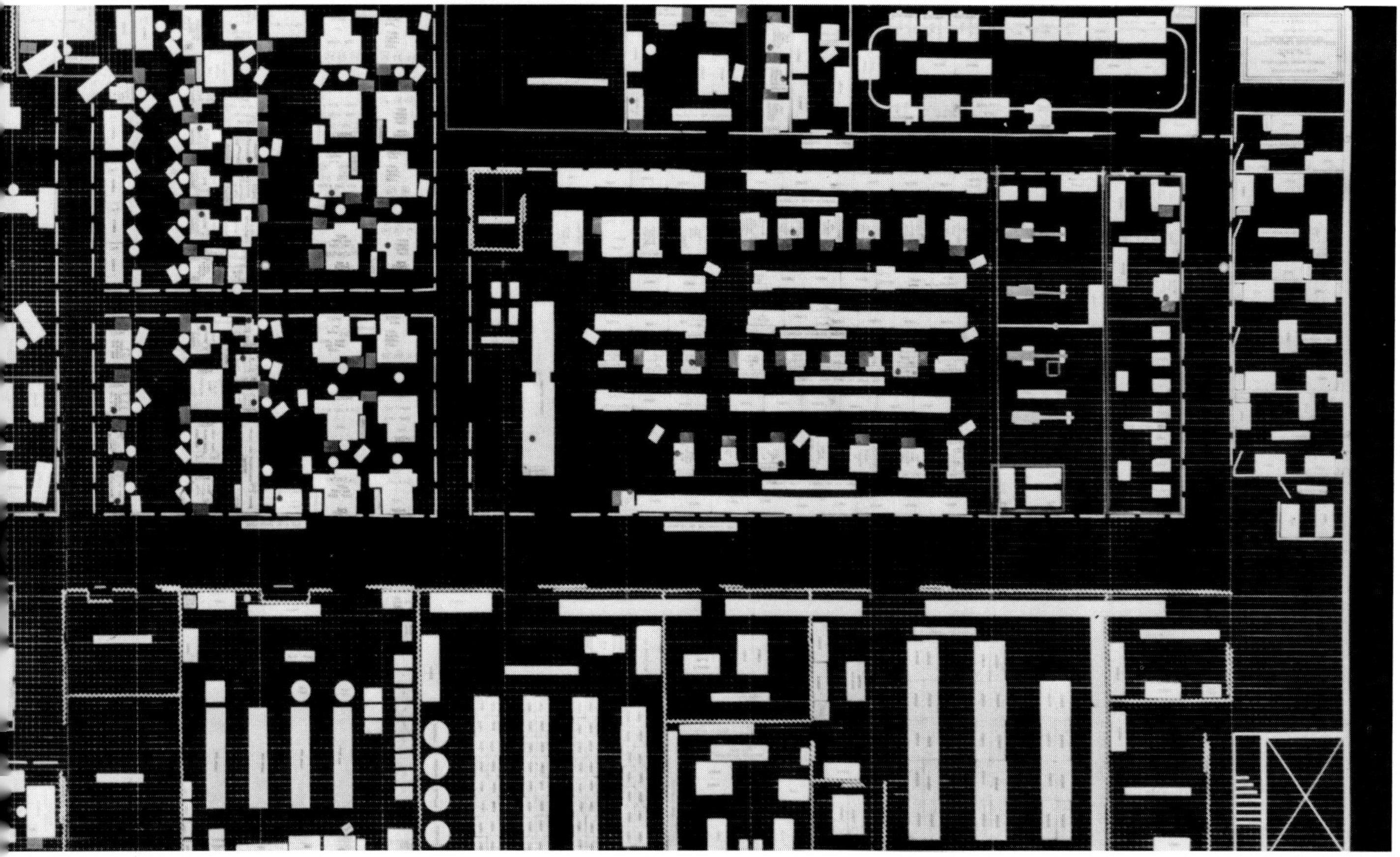

World War II

Guns

75mm M3 cannon layout. This gun was produced from April 25, 1942 to February 4, 1944. Buildings 34, 36 and 56 were used to produce the gun as well as the 76mm M1A2 cannon. The 76mm gun was produced through June 11, 1945. The 75mm gun was used in the M4 tank and the 76mm was used in the tank destroyer. The 75mm gun weighed 893 pounds and fired a projectile weighing 14.7 pounds. **Below**-Building 56 during construction work. The construction was only the center section of the building. Later construction added the east and west sections. **Bottom**-Building 56 during machine installation.

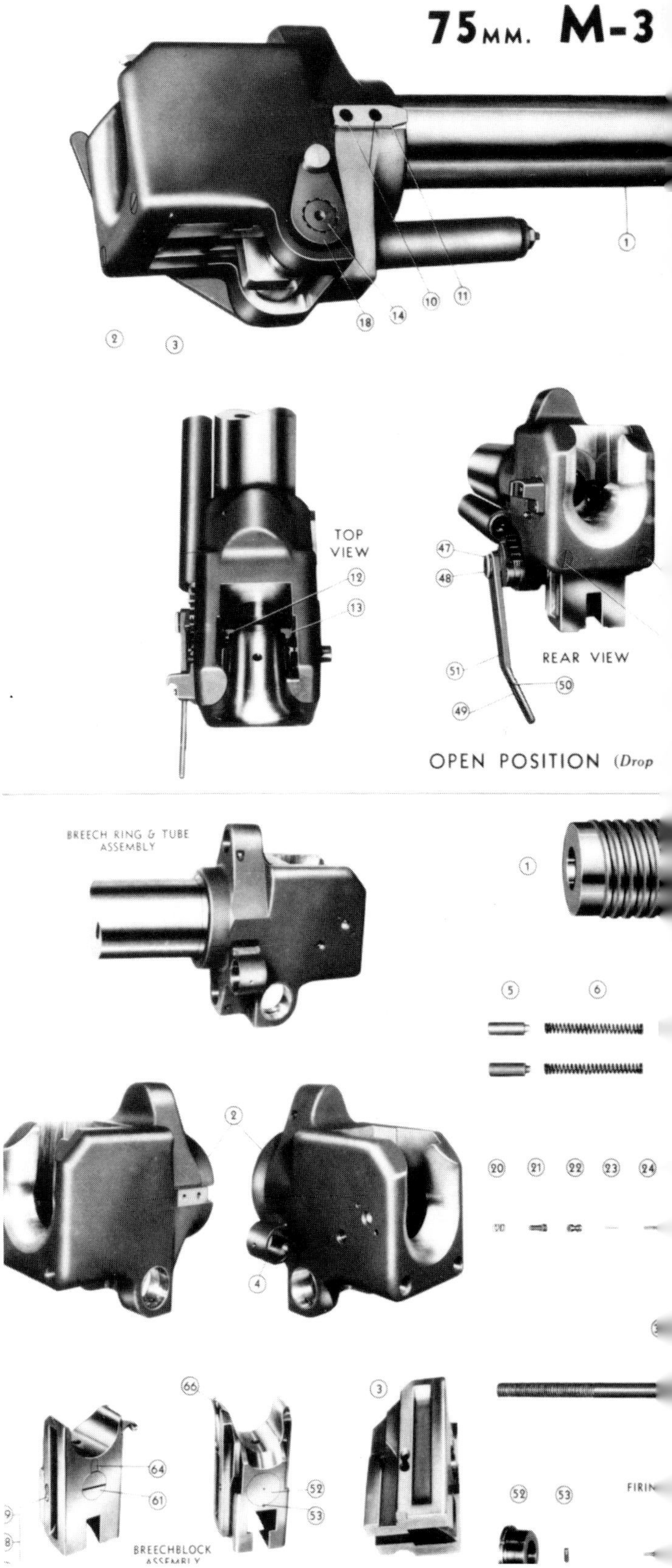

World War II

Guns

NON--OLDS MOTOR WORKS GUN DIVISION

CLOSED POSITION (*Firing*)

31

World War II

Guns

This page top left-Handling 75mm tubes into a lathe with a boom truck. **Top right**-Tube turning. **Bottom**-The Building 56 high bay machine floor.

Opposite page top-Turning threads on the big end of the gun. **Bottom**-Turning short tubes for the 75mm M-6 gun.

World War II

Guns

World War II

Guns

World War II

Guns

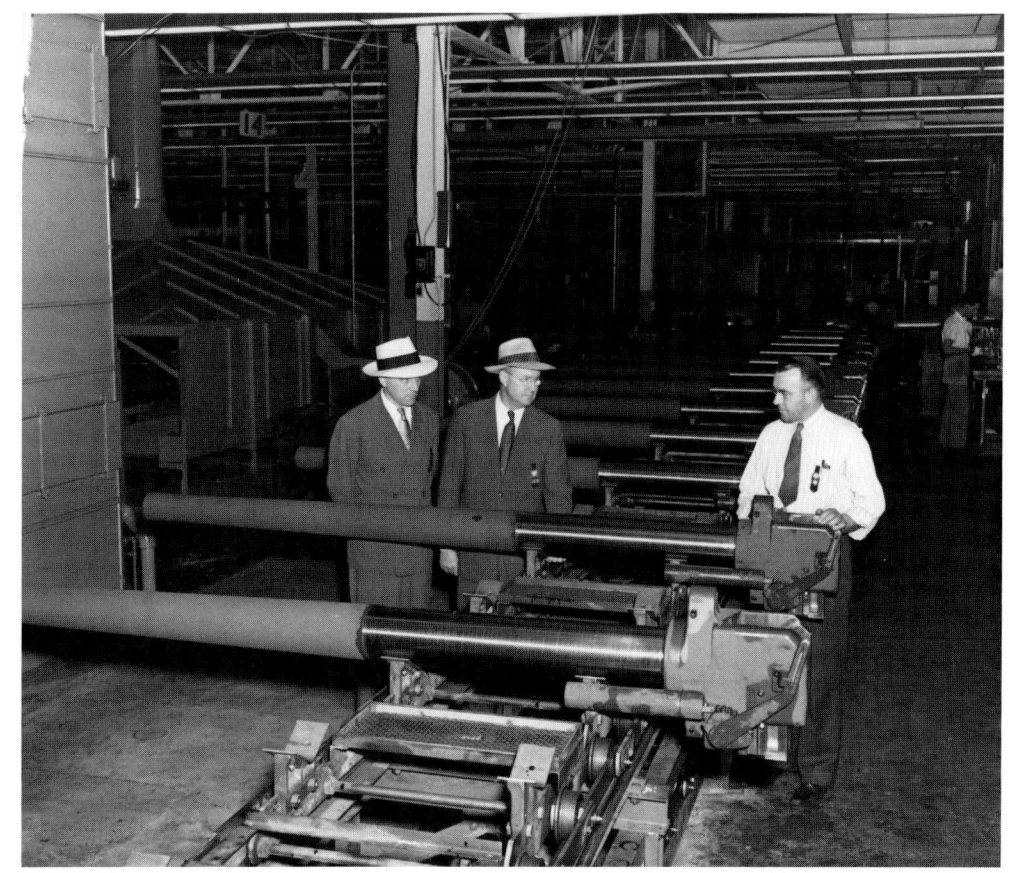

Opposite page top-Building 56 machine floor in the low bay area. **Bottom**-Tube straightening.

This page top-Gun assembly in Bldg. 36. John Dykstra, manufacturing manager (L), D. E. Ralston, acting general manager and an unidentified man look at a 75mm cannon. **Bottom**-Painting the guns. Shown is drying oven. Note the heat source is from heat lamps.

35

Guns

Right-Ed Lindner packing guns for shipment to the government. Notice how the hook holding the gun is covered with a soft material to protect the gun in handling. **Below**- A group of visitors at gun assembly. R. E. Griffin, Olds production manager, is in the white hat on the left.

World War II

Guns

Left-Machining breech rings. Breech rings were almost solid and were very heavy. **Below**-Broaching the breech ring faces.

World War II

Guns

Above-A good many visitors came to the plant to view our operations including the end of the cannon assembly line. R. E. Griffin, production manager, center with the hat. **Right**-The M4 tank with our 75mm cannon.

World War II

Guns

When a General Sherman M4 tank arrived at the plant, everyone wanted to see how the Olds 75mm cannon fit into the unit. Many of these employees had never seen a real tank. The white structures in the top photo are the gun test building.

World War II

Guns

World War II

Guns

Opposite page top-On February 12, 1943 Olds produced its 10,000th cannon with a celebration. **Bottom**-Gun assembly in Bldg. 36. Note the two size guns, the 75mm in the foreground and the 76mm in the back.
This page top-A 75mm gun display. **Below**-An outdoor display for the public. Note the children really looking things over.

World War II

Guns

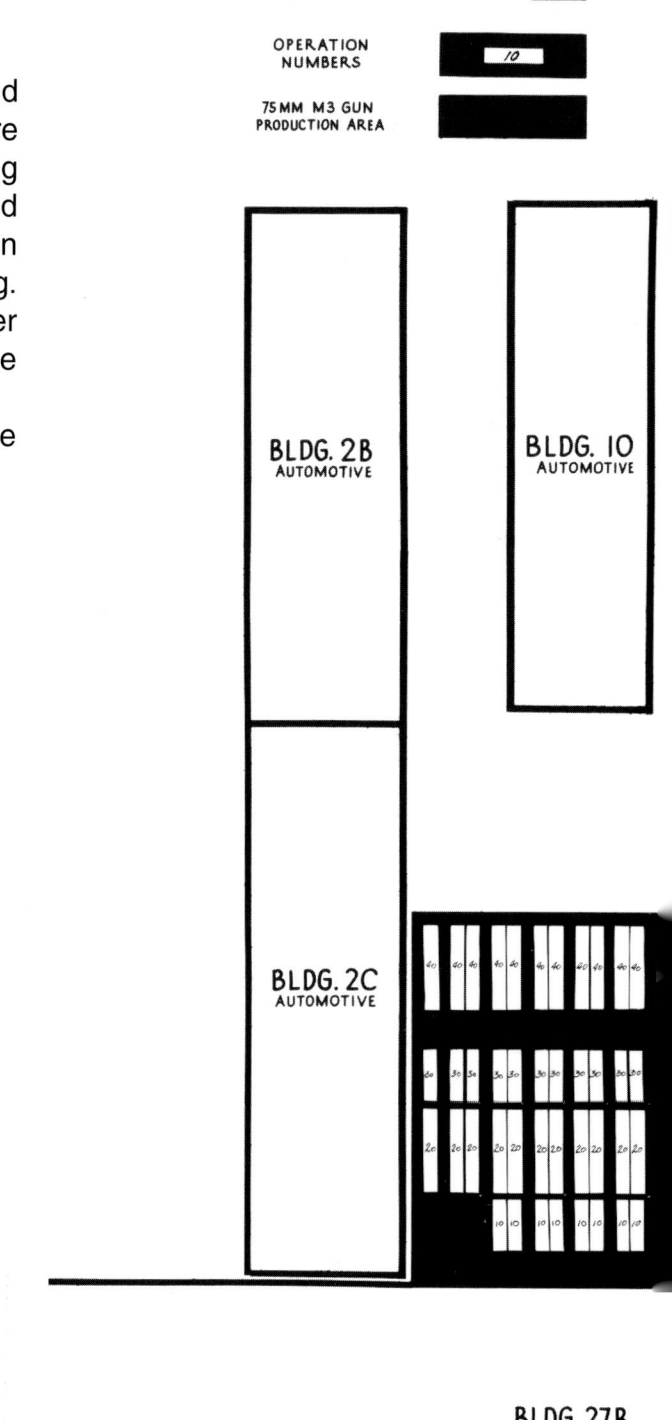

The 75mm gun layout in Buildings 36, 38, 40, 50, 52 and 56 as it was planned in October 1941. Gun tubes were scheduled to be manufactured starting in Bldg. 56 flowing through Bldgs. 50, 52 and into Bldg. 36. Breech rings and tubes would be transported through the railroad dock on the west into the assembly area at the north end of Bldg. 38. Bldg. 40 produced breech blocks. This plan was never implemented, however. The layout on the following page became the actual arrangement.

Below-Type of shells fired in a 75mm cannon also made at Olds.

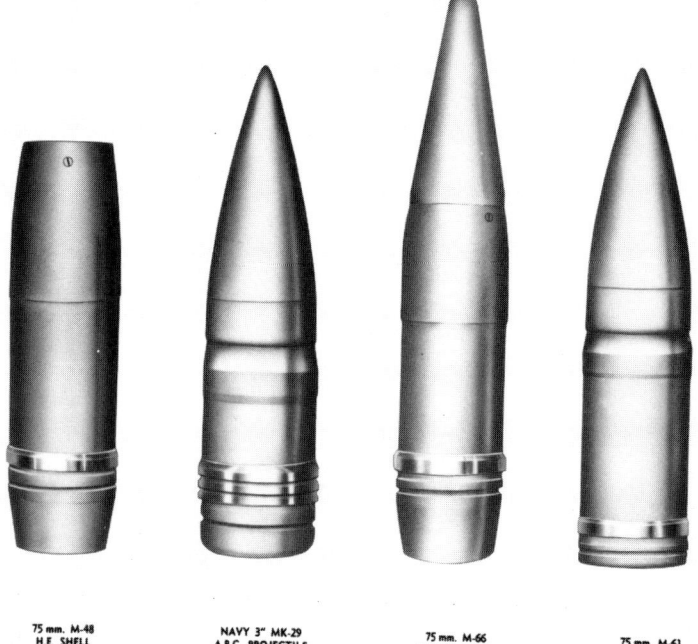

75 mm. M-48 H.E. SHELL — NAVY 3" MK-29 A.P.C. PROJECTILE — 75 mm. M-66 H.E.A.T. SHELL — 75 mm. M-61 A.P.C. PROJECTILE

World War II

Guns

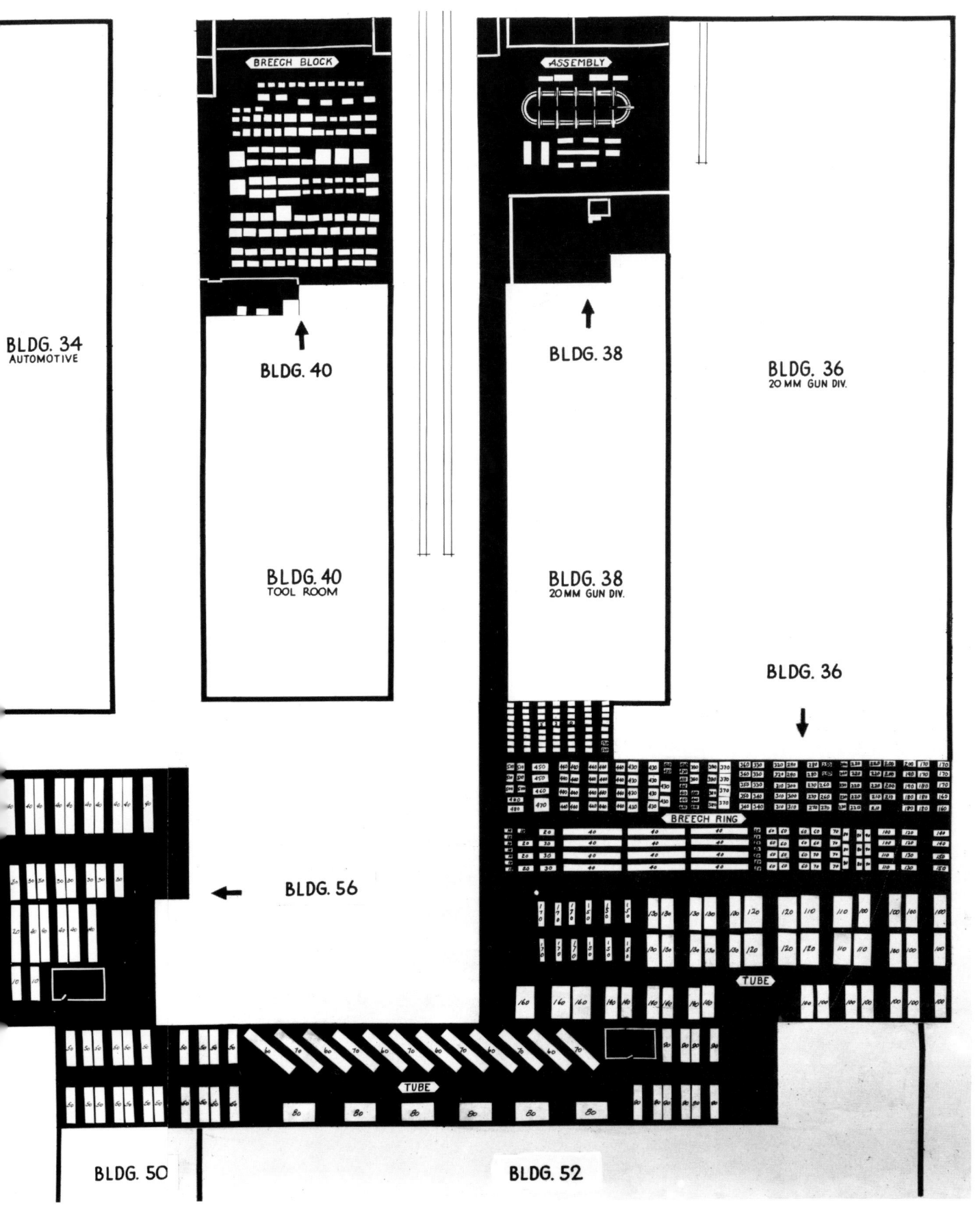

43

World War II

Guns

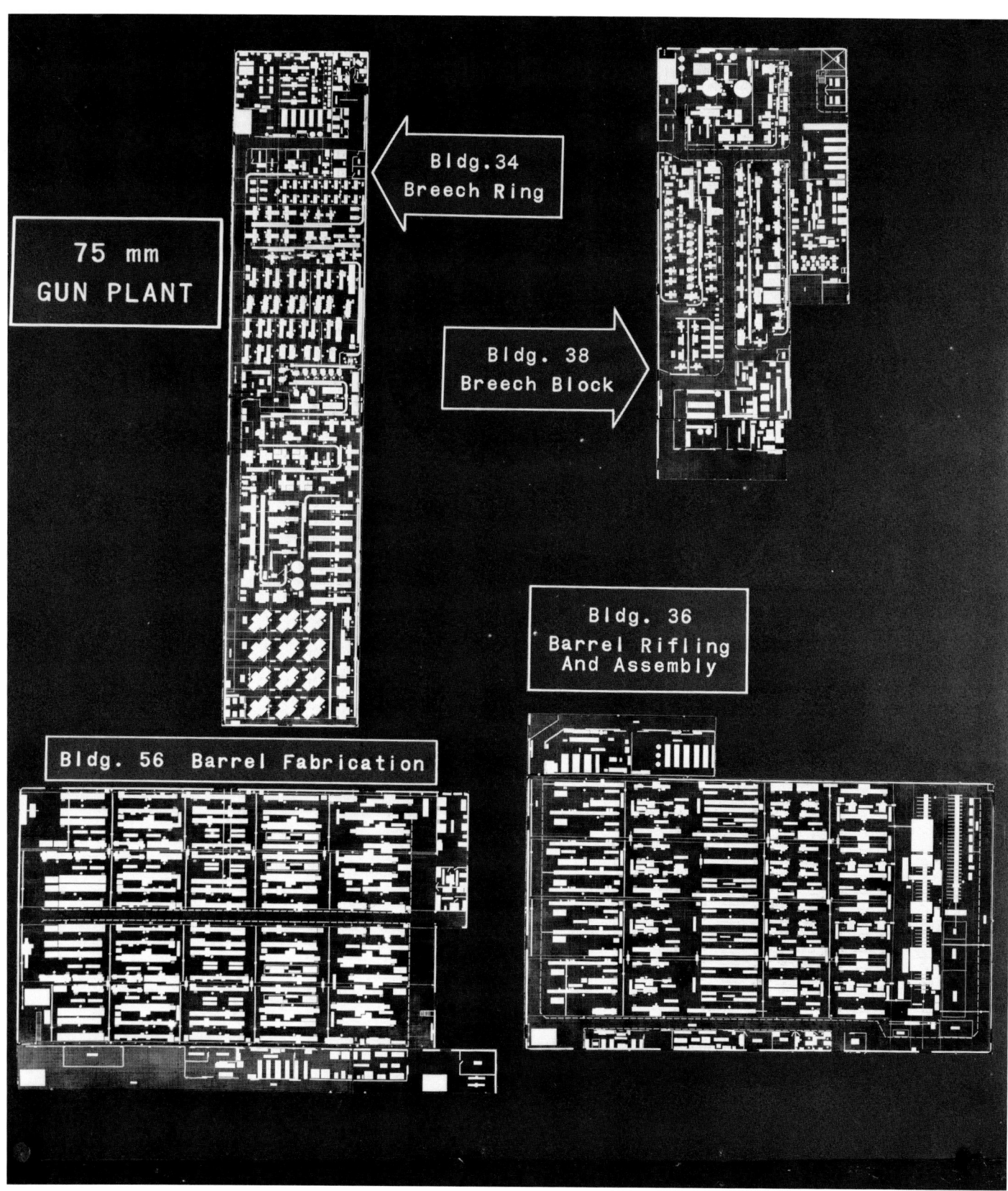

World War II

Guns

Opposite page-Building 56 area layout.
This page-Shown is the makeup of the three guns we were making. You will note in all cases Olds manufactured only the three main components, barrel, receiver and bolt for the 20mm gun; barrel, breech ring and breech block for the 75mm gun and tube (barrel), tube extension and lock frame for the 37mm gun.

GUN PRODUCTION ORGANIZATION

	20 MM	75 MM	37 MM	TOTAL
NO. OF DIFFERENT PARTS IN GUN	132	69	272	473
PARTS MANUFACTURED BY PRIME CONTRACTOR	3	3	3	9
PARTS MANUFACTURED BY SUB CONTRACTOR	129	66	269	464
NO. OF SUB CONTRACTORS	58	34	63	155

NET NO. OF 125 SUB CONTRACTORS DISTRIBUTED IN - - - - - 49 CITIES - - - 11 STATES

MACHINE TOOLS

		20 MM	75 MM	37 MM	TOTAL
PURCHASED	PRIME CONTRACTOR	329	602	140	1,071
	SUB CONTRACTOR	-	-	33	33
	TOTAL	329	602	173	1,104
CONVERTED	PRIME CONTRACTOR	183	215	135	533
	SUB CONTRACTOR	1,050	292	1,500	2,842
	TOTAL	1,233	507	1,635	3,375
% OF TOTAL CONVERTED		78.9	45.7	90.4	75.4

RAW MATERIAL

	20 MM	75 MM	37 MM
RAW MATERIAL PER GUN (POUNDS)	381	1,304	869
TYPES OF STEEL	24	17	13
NO. OF STEEL SIZES	99	43	170
NO. OF MATERIAL SOURCES	24	12	11

FLOOR SPACE

	20 MM	75 MM	37 MM
EXISTING	142,080 SQ. FT.	207,572 SQ. FT.	59,340 SQ. FT.
NEW	-	-	-

World War II

Shells

Shell production began at the GM Forge Plant #1 (Plant 2) first with the 75mm M48 shell on April 8, 1941 and the 105mm M1 shell on April 25, 1941. Buildings 32-75 at the current Plant 1 site were named GM Forge Plant #2. Production started here with the 75mm M72 shell on May 1, 1942. Both sites made a variety of shells following these beginnings. In addition, Janesville, WI and Kansas City, KS produced shells starting July 7, 1942 and August 19, 1941 respectively. **Below**-Photo shows a variety of shells produced at the four sites. By the time the war ended, Lansing had produced 10 different shells, Janesville six and Kansas City eight. Some sizes were produced at more than one site, i.e. 105mm M1 at both Lansing and Janesville. **Bottom**-This Layout shows the Bldg. 32-75 area as it was arranged for production of 75mm shells. Eventually, Bldg. 32 would become the production area for the 155mm M101 shell. This would be the largest and most difficult shell produced at Lansing.

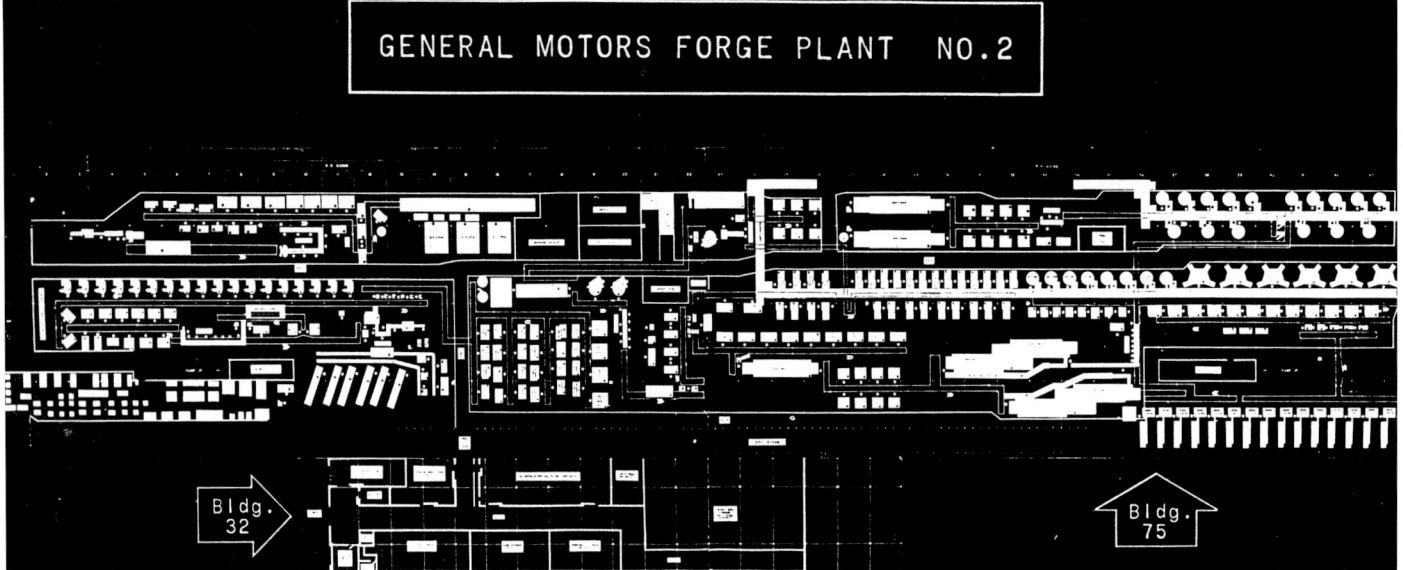

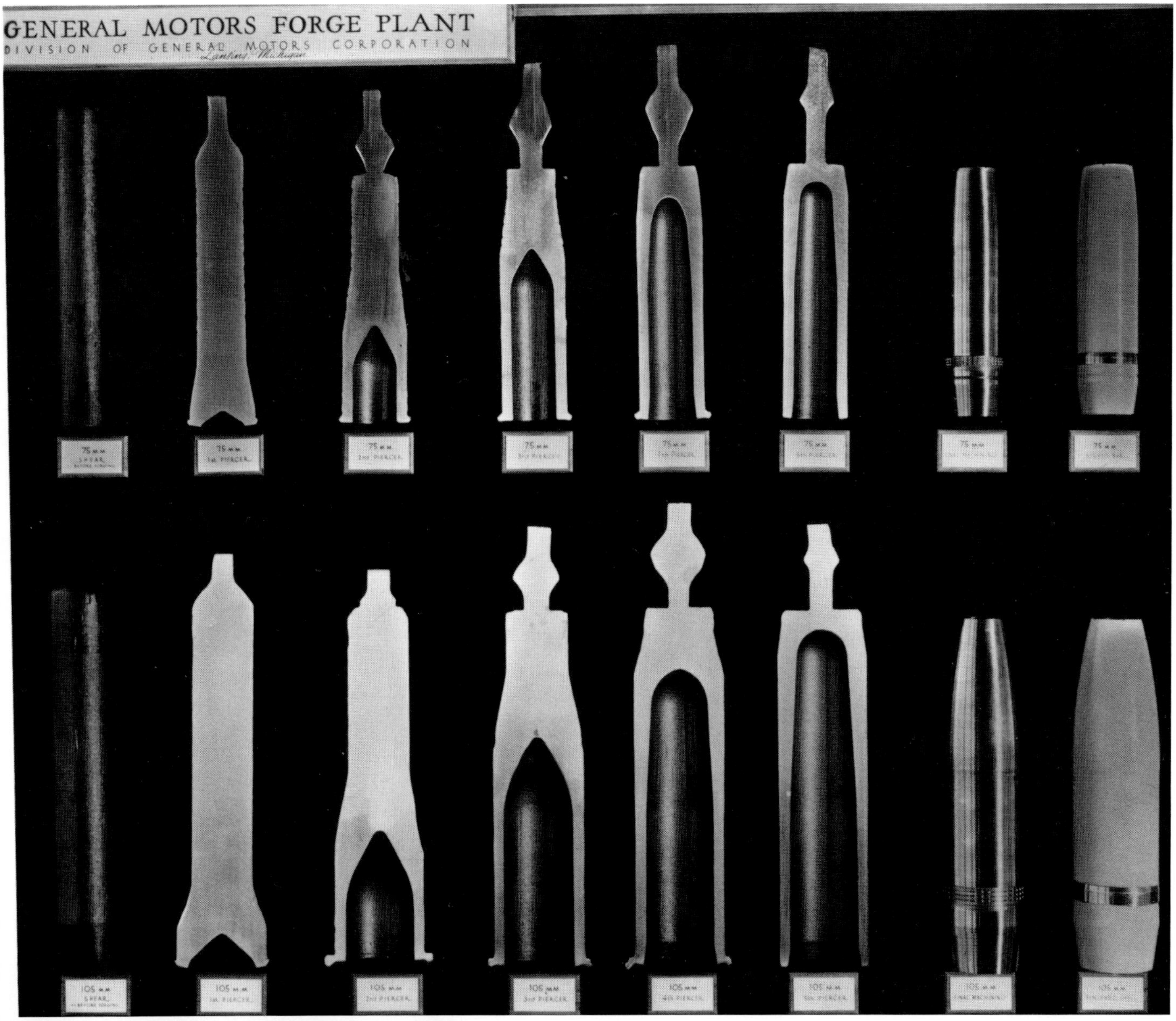

World War II
Shells

Above-Many of the shells required forging work. Shown are typical forging passes needed to produce the 75mm shell (top) and 105mm shell using an upsetter. The shell is formed with each successive pass until it is ready for machining.

Left-Operator is handling a hot forging billet in preparation for starting the forging process. The tongs used were held closed by the ring on the tong handles. The hook above was connected to a balancer which supported some of the weight. It still took a fairly strong person to handle the larger billets. The operator would start at the top of the die and drop down with each cycle of the upsetter. This would progressively change the shape of the hot shell into the final forged part.

Shells — World War II

This page top-Machining a 105mm shell. **Center**-Rotating band installation area for the 105mm shell. **Bottom left**-105mm shell deburring and inspection line. **Bottom right**-75mm inspection line.

Opposite page top left-75mm heat treat furnace with a load of shells. **Top right**-75mm shell inspection and repair area. **Bottom**-Laura Morton and Otto Baumann, Forge Plant employees, with several racks of finished shells. Note the plant badge on the man's collar and the center pin on his cap. The pin is the "E" award pin given to every employee after Olds received the first "E" award August 10, 1942

World War II

Shells

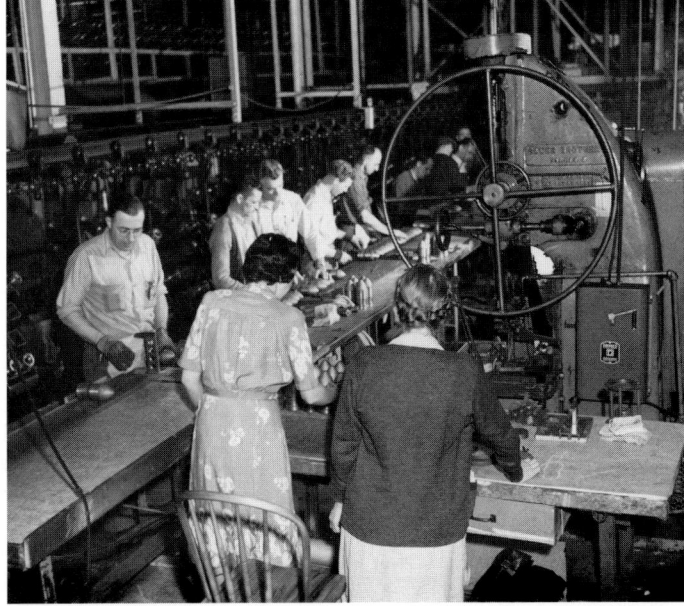

Shells World War II

This page right-105mm inspection line. Note all the inspectors are women. **Below left**-Two women operate a shell machining operation. **Below right**-Oldsmobile began making 155mm shells on October 5, 1944. Schedule shows period from October 9 to October 27. You will note we are behind schedule by 3442 shells by October 19th. The 155 was a very difficult shell to make. It took considerable effort to achieve the production schedule but we eventually would do so.

Opposite page top-Machining floor for the 155mm shell. **Bottom left**-Centering the 155 shell. **Right center**-Loading the shell into the first lathe operation. Note the tongs used to handle the heavy billet. **Right bottom**-The turning operation used a heavy cutting oil which came out of pipes in front of the operator.

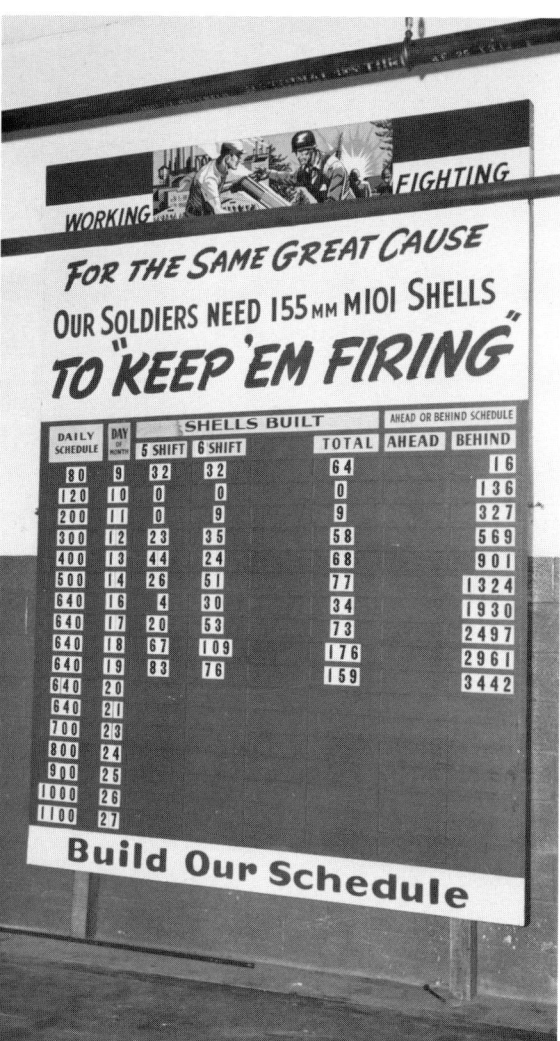

50

World War II

Shells

Shells

World War II

This page top-A large press was used for nosing the end of the 155mm shell. **Bottom**-Much of the machining for shells was lathe turning. Here's one of the many areas that turned a portion of the shell. Note the front employee checking his work with a pair of micrometers.

Opposite page top left-After the shells were heat treated, more turning was required. **Top right**-Additional turning operations. Note the women in this photo and **bottom** photo. The roller conveyor helped in the handling of the heavy shells. Lila Miller, Viola Buerge and Harry Johnson are doing the machining.

World War II

Shells

Shells

Above-Machining the 155 mm shell. Note the area on the shell that appears rough. This spot on the shell is covered by a copper band called the rotating band. It is used to help control the shell as it is fired by allowing the rifling to spin the shell. The copper minimizes the wear on the gun barrel as the shell slides through the barrel

Right-Oral Bigelow installs the copper rotating band. This machine would squeeze the copper band into the mating groove on the shell.

World War II

Shells

Above-Once the copper band was installed it was necessary to turn it to size and shape. A group of lathes does the turning.

Left-The final operation prior to packing and shipping was to paint the shell with traditional army green. Charles Krathwohl completes this operation.

Shells

World War II

Above-Shell display made by Exhibit and Display. A great variety of displays were made for both public and employee viewing. This display shows the types of shells. Production floor and war scene photos were used to tie production to the war front which at times seemed far away.

Right-Display shows shells with their brass casings.

World War II

Shells

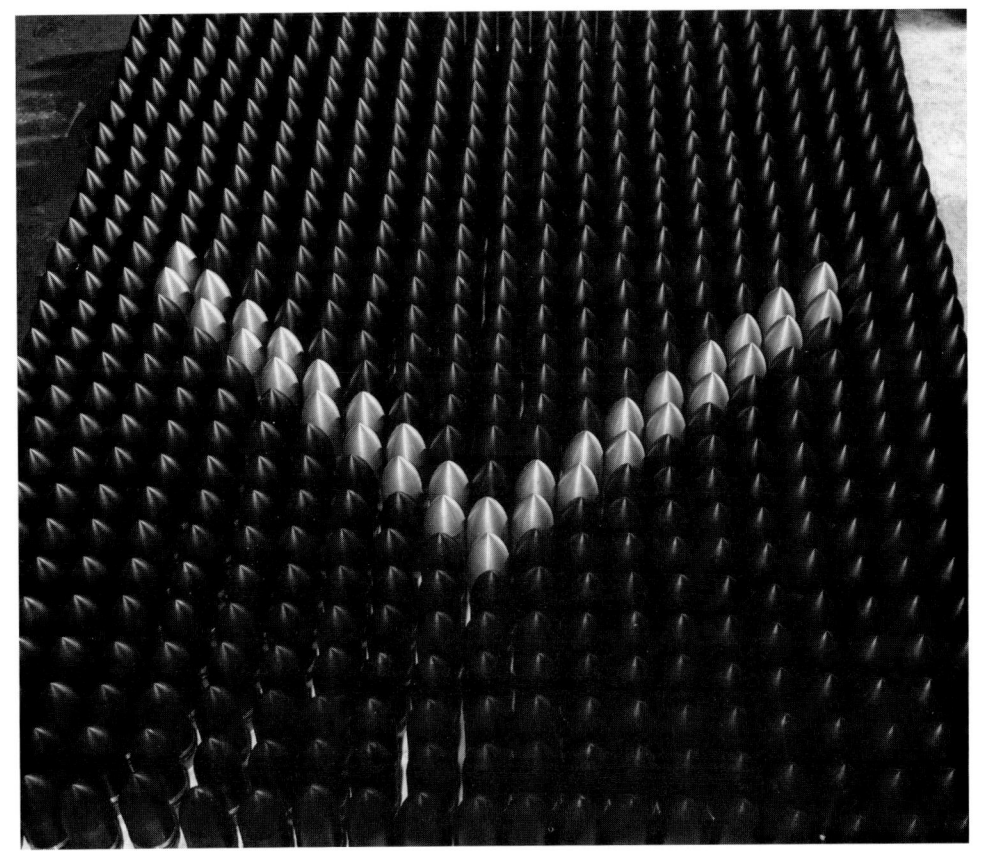

Left-The "V" for victory slogan used during the war. Here some of the 75mm shells are used to show that famous letter.

Below-Wooden case displaying shells stood in the general manager's lobby in Building 60 (Administration Building) during the war. In the lower left corner is one of the rocket bodies made by Olds. The large shell in the middle with an eye in the top is a 155mm shell.

Misc.

World War II

3-INCH M-7 GUN..

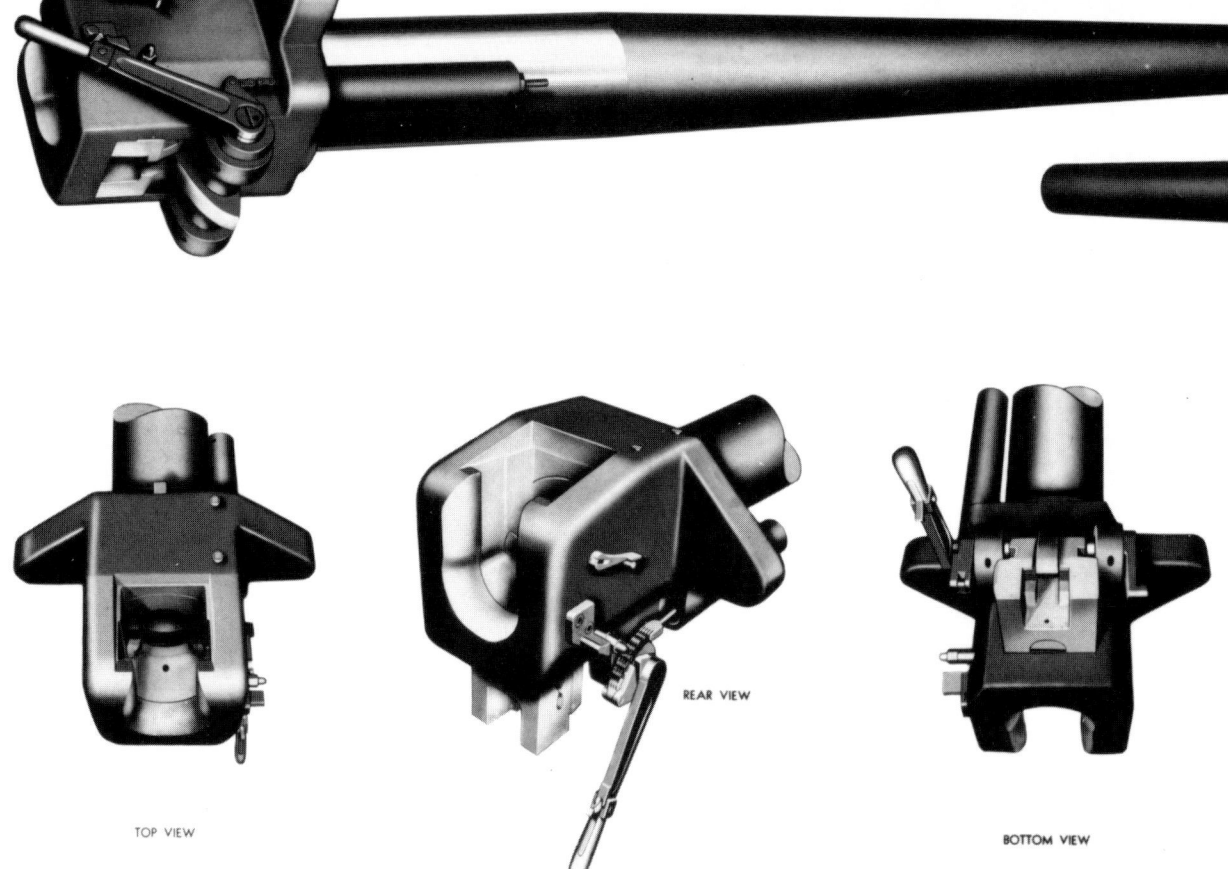

TOP VIEW

OPEN POSITION (Drop Block)

REAR VIEW

BOTTOM VIEW

World War II

Misc.

Opposite page top left-Much of the war activity involved lathe work so there were lots of tools to be sharpened to keep the production lines going. H. Sergeant demonstrates the proper way to sharpen carbide tools. **Top right**-Small press area. **This page left**-Although Olds produced a great variety of war materiel, many of the parts were purchased from outside suppliers. Shown is receiving inspection area where parts were checked to verify that specifications were met. **Below**-3" M7 gun layout. This gun was very similar to the 76mm M1A2 gun.

DSMOBILE GUN DIVISION

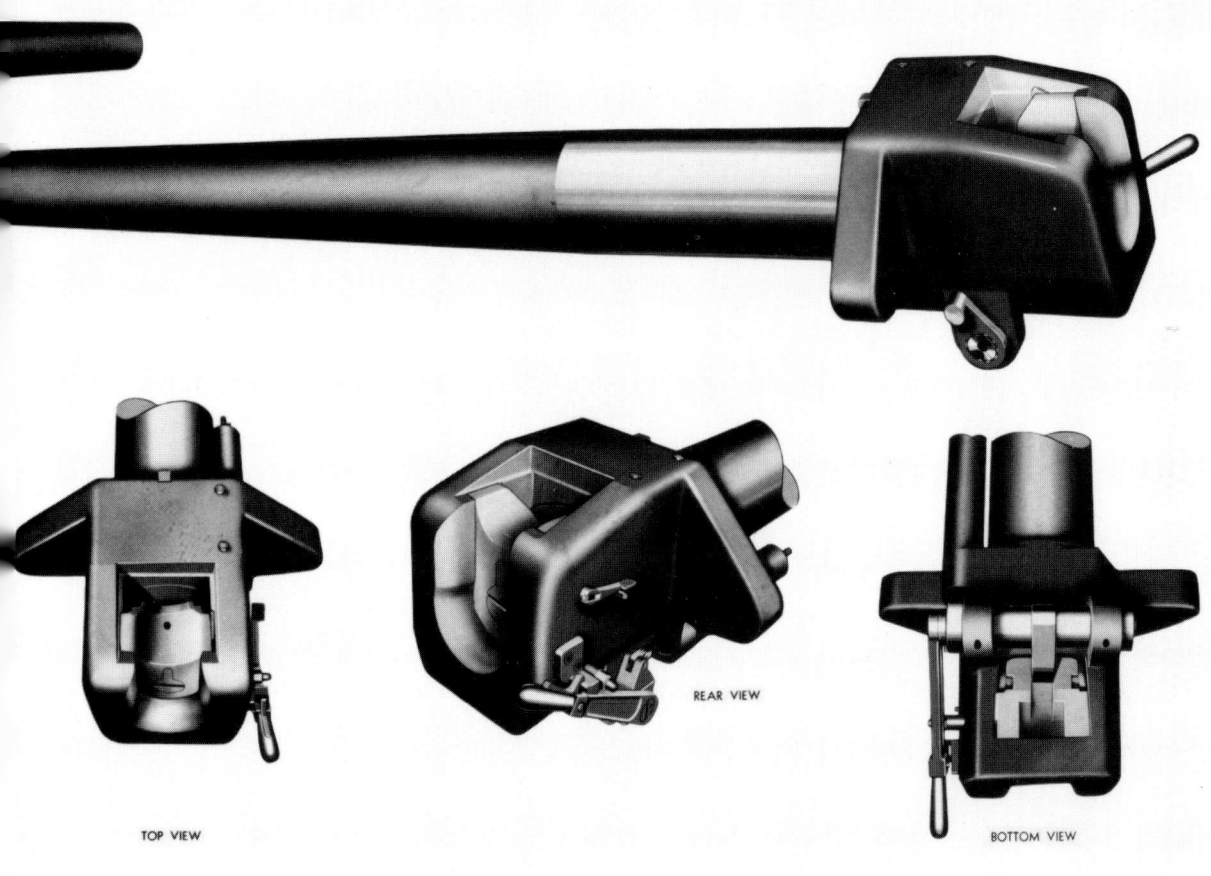

CLOSED POSITION (Firing)

World War II

Rods

Olds received a contract for Pratt and Whitney radial engine connecting rods. Production began April 15, 1944 and ended June 17, 1945. This job was unique. The rod was machined all over. In the final stages of production the rod had to be handled with gloves to avoid leaving fingerprints which would cause rust. **Below**-Production chart shows we were having production problems as early as May. This type of sign was used in the plant so employees would understand the needs and could see how we were doing.

Opposite page top-The machining floor in Bldg. 33. **Bottom**-Much of the work was done by tool room milling machines. Roland Eckhart and Walter Konen (R) do the work here. Note the wooden boxs with separators for each rod to minimize nicks and scratches on the machined surfaces.

World War II

Rods

World War II

Rods

World War II

Rods

Opposite page top left-A gang milling machine machining four rods at a time. **Top right**-Single spindle mills machining four rods at a time. **Bottom**-A. Sermak and John Granstrom check the accuracy of a milling cut.

This page top-Each rod was heat treated during the manufacturing process. **Left**-Polishing a rod. Any nicks or scratches had to be buffed out before shipment.

World War II

Cranks

Olds produced crankshafts for the Rolls Royce Merlin aircraft engine which powered the P-51 Mustang fighter. Building 33 was used for this activity. The engine was a V-12 with hollow main and rod bearings. Production was first announced in May 1944.

This page right-Boring the holes in the main and rod bearings. **Below**-Drilling the oil holes.

Opposite page top left-A group viewing the crank floor. **Top right**-Machining bearings. **Bottom**-Dewey Fuller polishing bearings. Dewey had four sons in the services.

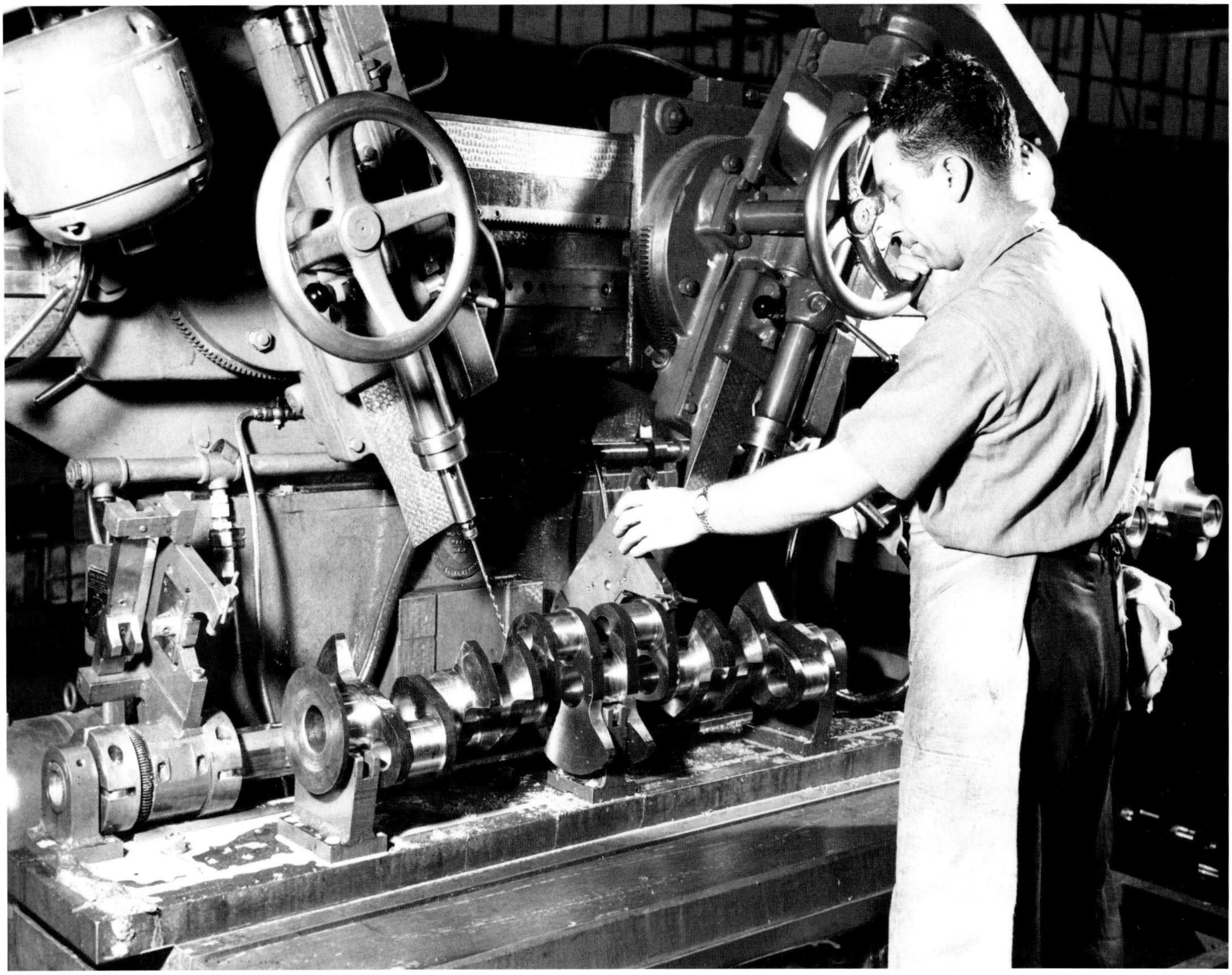

World War II

Cranks

World War II

Rockets

In September 1944 production started on the 4.5" T22 rocket. Over 240,000 were made. Building 75 was used for this operation.

Opposite page-Rocket schedule for the first few days of production shows Olds was ahead of schedule.

This page top-Loading the rocket coating machine. **Left**-Dark photo shows the press used to cold form portions of the body. **Below**-The finished product being inspected.

World War II

Gun Test

68

World War II

Gun Test

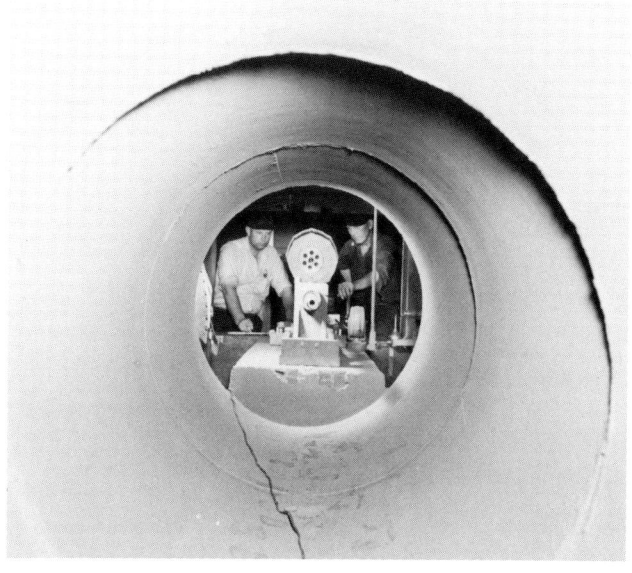

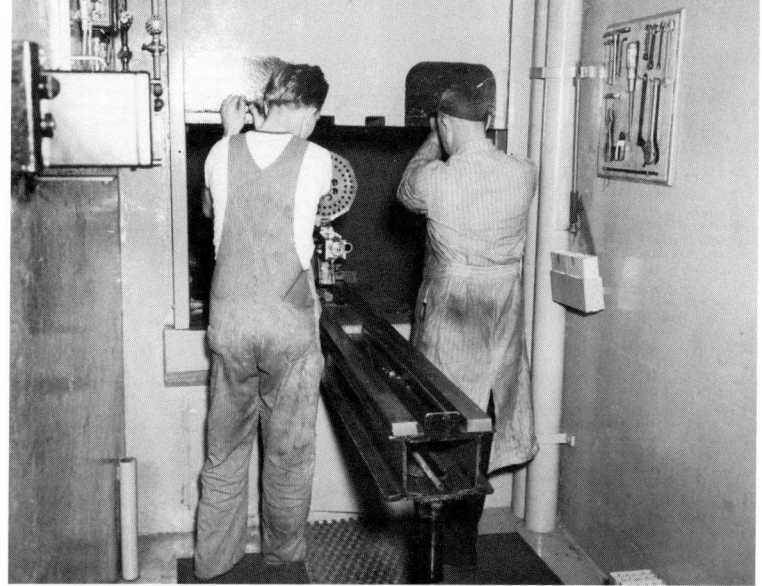

All 20mm guns were tested under firing conditions. To do this, an underground test facility (Building 44) was built north of Bldg. 36. Two above ground buildings housed the access to the firing chamber and the backstop. Large tubes connected the two locations. The guns were fired from the firing chamber with the bullets travelling down the tubes to the backstop. There were nine firing stations. However, usually only two or three guns were fired at a time. The noise was extremely bad.

The photos on these two pages show the underground firing room and the tube looking toward the barrel end of the gun.

This page bottom-A 37mm gun in firing position. 37mm guns had considerably more destructive force than the 20mm gun.

The outside of the gun test range can be seen in several of the outdoor photos shown on pages 122, 152 and 167.

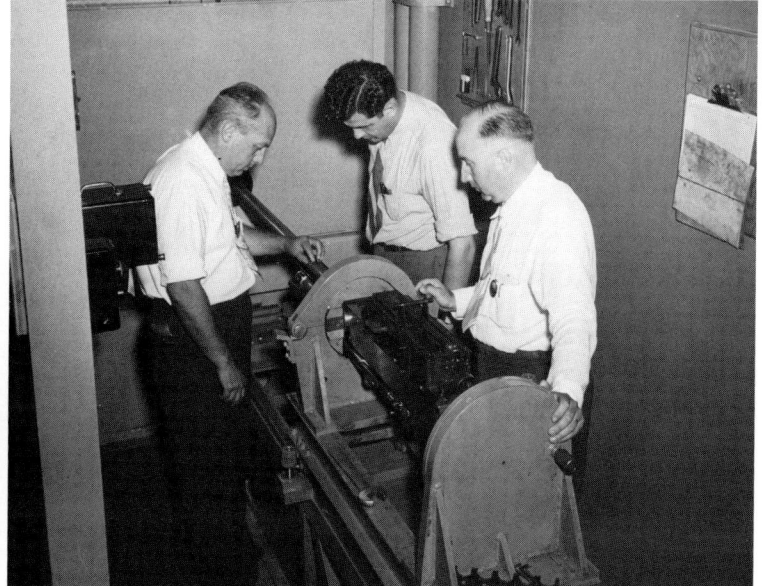

World War II

The Forge Plant

The GM Forge Plant #1 (Forge Plant, Plant 2, Craft Centre) layout in the early part of the war. Buildings 1, 2, 3 and 4 would later become buildings 201, 202, 203 and 204. These Buildings would be expanded considerably through the addition of Buildings 206, 207 and 208. Although difficult to read, this layout shows several interesting features. The large white area at the top is steel storage in the yard. Building 1 houses the offices, maintenance and tool and die room activities. The round machines in Buildings 2 and 3 are furnaces for heating billets for forging. Building 2 houses the upsetters lined up along the bottom of that building, with 105mm shell forging on the left and 75mm on the right. The tall vertical boxes are heat treat furnaces. Machining for the 75mm shell is on the right side of Building 4 with the 105mm on the left.

Below-The Forge Plant from the northeast.

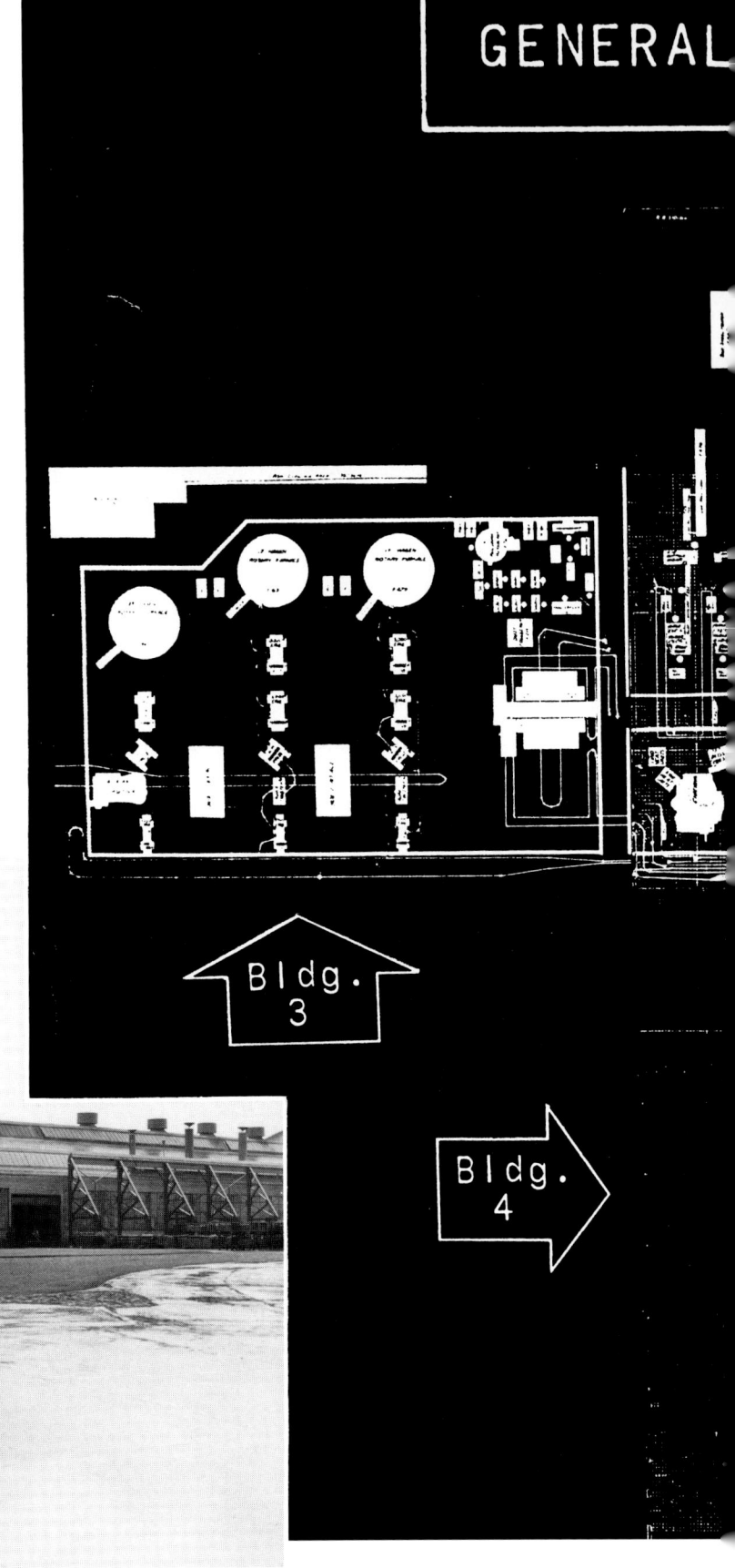

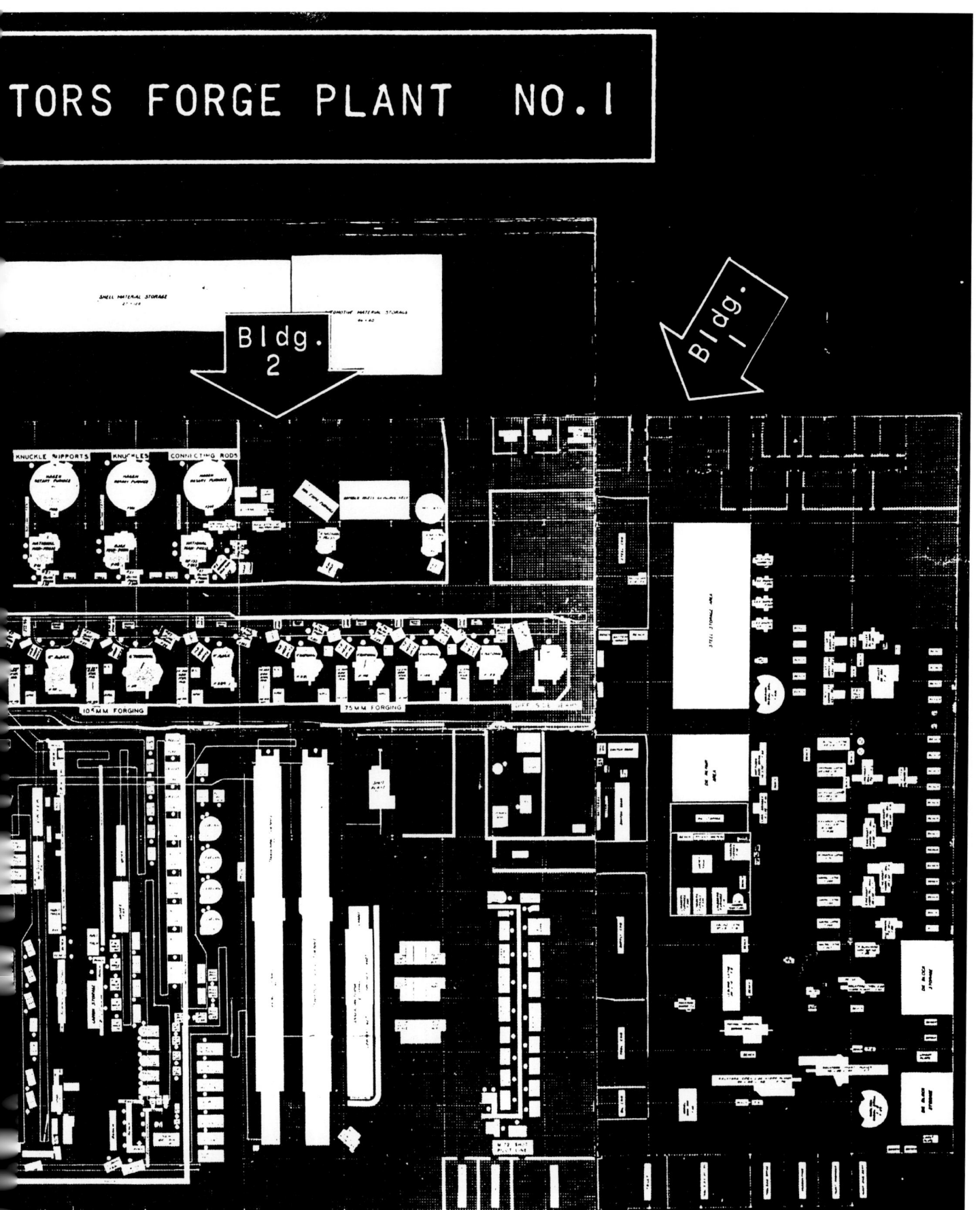

The Forge Plant

World War II

This page right-Forging a large billet. **Below**-A billet being handled with long tongs.

Opposite page top-An employee loading billets into a furnace. **Bottom**-A crew forming a hot billet.

World War II

The Forge Plant

The Forge Plant

World War II

This page top-William Betts removing a landing gear part from the furnace. **Below**-Leo Barnhart (L) and Frank Valek blocking a propeller part. **Below right**-Leslie Waite (L) and George McCumby making a prop spider. **Bottom**-John Freeman forging a cannon breech casing body trunnion.

Opposite page top-Glenn Newman removing a bomber landing gear fork from the furnace. **Bottom**-Leo Taylor forming a part on a hammer.

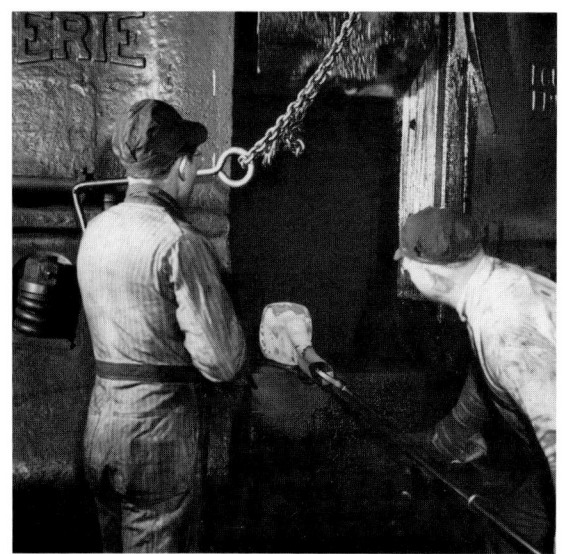
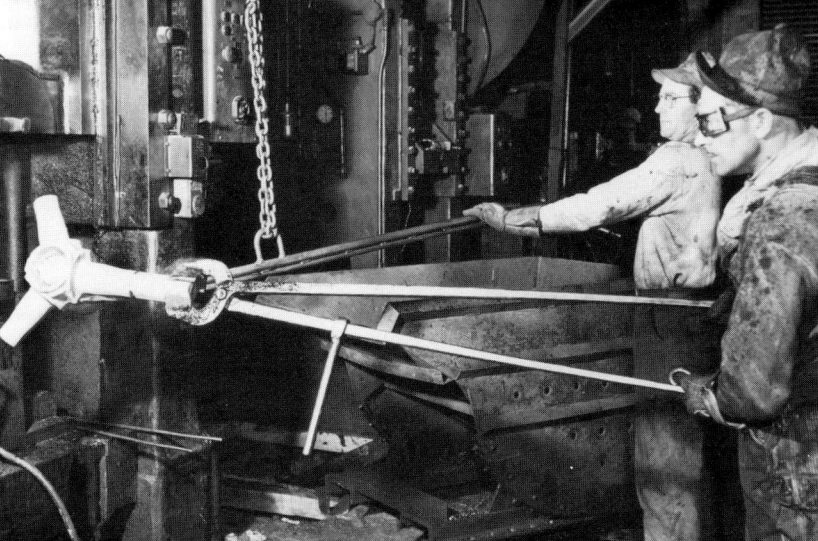

World War II

The Forge Plant

The Forge Plant — World War II

Some of the forging operations on these two pages and the previous two were done with Erie steam drop hammers. You will note Erie in several photos. Other forging was done with large presses. The photos on these pages show a variety of parts forged at the GM Forge Plant #1 (Plant 2). These range from hubs and prop spiders to heavy landing gear parts. Note the special tongs and methods of balancing the different parts. Also note the heavy clothing, gloves and eye protection worn. Wool underwear was worn by most of the employees. The Forge Plant was a rather noisy and dirty place. Many of the forging operations took considerable skill. It was however, one big family. **This page above**-John Pierce machining a die. It took a good many dies to forge all the parts made. **Bottom**-Group watching a hub forging operation. C. B. Dakin, plant manager is the third person from the left.

The dark photo on the **opposite page** is of the clean and finish area. These men are grinding off flash from a large landing gear cylinder.

World War II

The Forge Plant

77

World War II

The Forge Plant

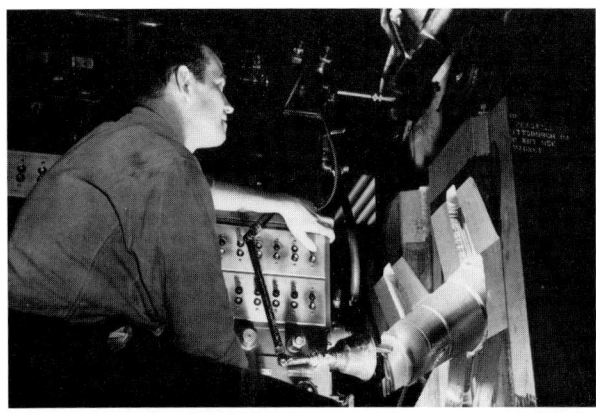

World War II

The Forge Plant

Opposite page top left-Charles Howell machining a die on a Keller die sinking machine. This is in the die room. **Top right**-A die being ground in the forging hammer. **Left Center**-Dies were held in place with a large key. These men are using a steel battering ram to drive in a key. **Bottom**-In August 1944, after Building 207 was built, a special open house was held in the yard for servicemen travelling through the area. Note the armored carrier and servicemen on the stage.

This page top-An Exhibit and Display Department array of the different parts made at the plant. **Bottom**-The skill of steam hammer operators is demonstrated here as Dave Taylor cracks an egg without breaking it.

World War II

Advertising

Even though the war was going on, Olds advertised regularily. The ads shown here are typical of those used during that era.

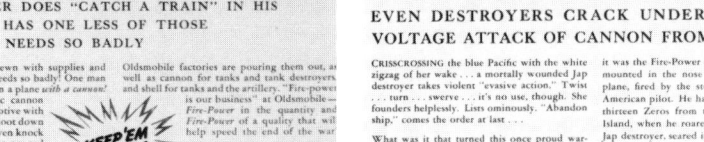

World War II

Advertising

The ads demonstrated our commitment to the war effort and kept Oldsmobile in the public eye.

Pugnacious Pup!

OFFICIAL INSIGNE 355TH FIGHTER SQUADRON ARMY AIR FORCES

To the men who fly into battle with this emblem on their Airacobra fighter planes—and to those other squadron members who do their work on the ground—Oldsmobile respectfully dedicates this page.

Here's to those "Pugnacious Pups," the "Battling Bulldogs" of the 355th Fighter Squadron. We know that whatever they do—whether in practice or in actual combat—they'll do it with all the tenacity and savage courage for which the bulldog is famous. Let the Axis beware, when these fighting Yanks come streaking from a cloud cover, their motors roaring, their cannon blasting out a stream of high-explosive destruction... We at Oldsmobile wish every member of the 355th Fighter Squadron the very best of luck against the enemy. May every "dogfight" be a winning fight... for the "Pugnacious Pups!"

FIRE-POWER is Our Business!

Nothing gives us greater satisfaction at Oldsmobile than the knowledge that the Fire-Power we build is being used by such gallant and courageous fighting men as those who represent America on the far flung battle-fronts today. Our automatic aircraft cannon, for example, are mounted on the planes of the "Pugnacious Pups," and many other famous squadrons of the A.A.F. Our tank and tank destroyer cannon are manned by the fighters of the Armored and Tank Destroyer Forces. Our high-explosive and armor-piercing shell are fired in almost every branch of the services, including the Field Artillery and the Navy. As we work at our machines and our benches and our drawing boards, putting every bit of skill and knowledge we can muster into the job... our chief hope is that the Fire-Power products we build may prove worthy of the fighting men who use them.

BACK THEM UP TO THE LIMIT

The closer our fighting men get to Tokyo and Berlin and the tougher the going becomes, the more they need the support of *our* fighting dollars. Let's not let them down.
BUY WAR BONDS

OLDSMOBILE DIVISION OF GENERAL MOTORS
KEEP 'EM FIRING

World War II

Advertising

Midnight Mauler
WITH A HIGH-EXPLOSIVE PUNCH!

New Douglas (P-70) Night Fighter has the *fire-power* of four 20 MM. cannon!

UP INTO the inky blackness of the night, straight and swift as an arrow to its target, a big new AAF fighter plane darts through the darkness, armed to the teeth with cannon! Searchlights fan out to help him. Watch!... they've caught an enemy raider in their glare. There's a roar, a blinding flash, an Axis bomber bursting into flames... another victim of the high-explosive barrage of this 4-barreled battery of fire-power!

Most details of the mysterious Douglas (P-70) Night Fighter are still a closely guarded secret. But this much our enemies know. One of the striking features of this "Midnight Mauler" is its armament of heavy-hitting artillery! The concentrated fire-power of four 20 mm. automatic cannon blazes away at one touch of the trigger! These are the same kind of long-range aircraft cannon that we of Oldsmobile are building for Army Ordnance, along with cannon for tanks and tank destroyers — shell for both Army and Navy.

Help fire this 4-cannon blast!

A plane like this fires high-explosive cannon shell at a rate of over 2000 a minute! That costs money — money which must come from us at home.

BUY WAR BONDS!

FIRE-POWER IS OUR BUSINESS!

OLDSMOBILE DIVISION OF GENERAL MOTORS
KEEP 'EM FIRING

World War II

Advertising

The Black Widow*
SNARES AN AXIS "FLY"!

*Black Widow is the name of America's newest, most deadly night fighter... the cannon-firing P-61

An Axis raider drones toward its target, unaware that far ahead... the Black Widow is waiting! Busy Axis hands prepare to release their cargo of destruction. Straining Axis eyes peer out into the night... where the Black Widow is waiting! But they see nothing, no sign of danger, until suddenly... a huge, dark shape appears from nowhere! There's a burst of cannon fire, a blinding explosion, an Axis plane flaming downward... the Black Widow has struck!

The P-61 Black Widow is the first American plane to be designed, from the very beginning, as a night fighter. It has *everything*... speed to catch an enemy unawares, electronic devices to search in the dark, fire-power enough to pulverize anything that flies!

Fire-power is our specialty at Oldsmobile. Automatic aircraft cannon, such as we have built by the tens of thousands, help give the Black Widow its "poisonous sting." Other Oldsmobile war products include cannon for tanks and tank destroyers, high-explosive and armor-piercing shell, parts for aircraft engines and heavy-duty military vehicles... plus other "censored" weapons which are already doing much to "Keep 'Em Firing!"

The Widow's MIGHT is Fire-Power!

The Black Widow packs the Fire-Power of fast-firing 20 mm. automatic aerial cannon that can smash any enemy plane that flies.

YOUR BONDS HELP PROVIDE IT

Give our fighting men the Fire-Power they need to fight with. Buy more War Bonds and Stamps to Keep 'Em Firing.

OLDSMOBILE DIVISION OF GENERAL MOTORS
FIRE-POWER IS OUR BUSINESS!

World War II

Advertising

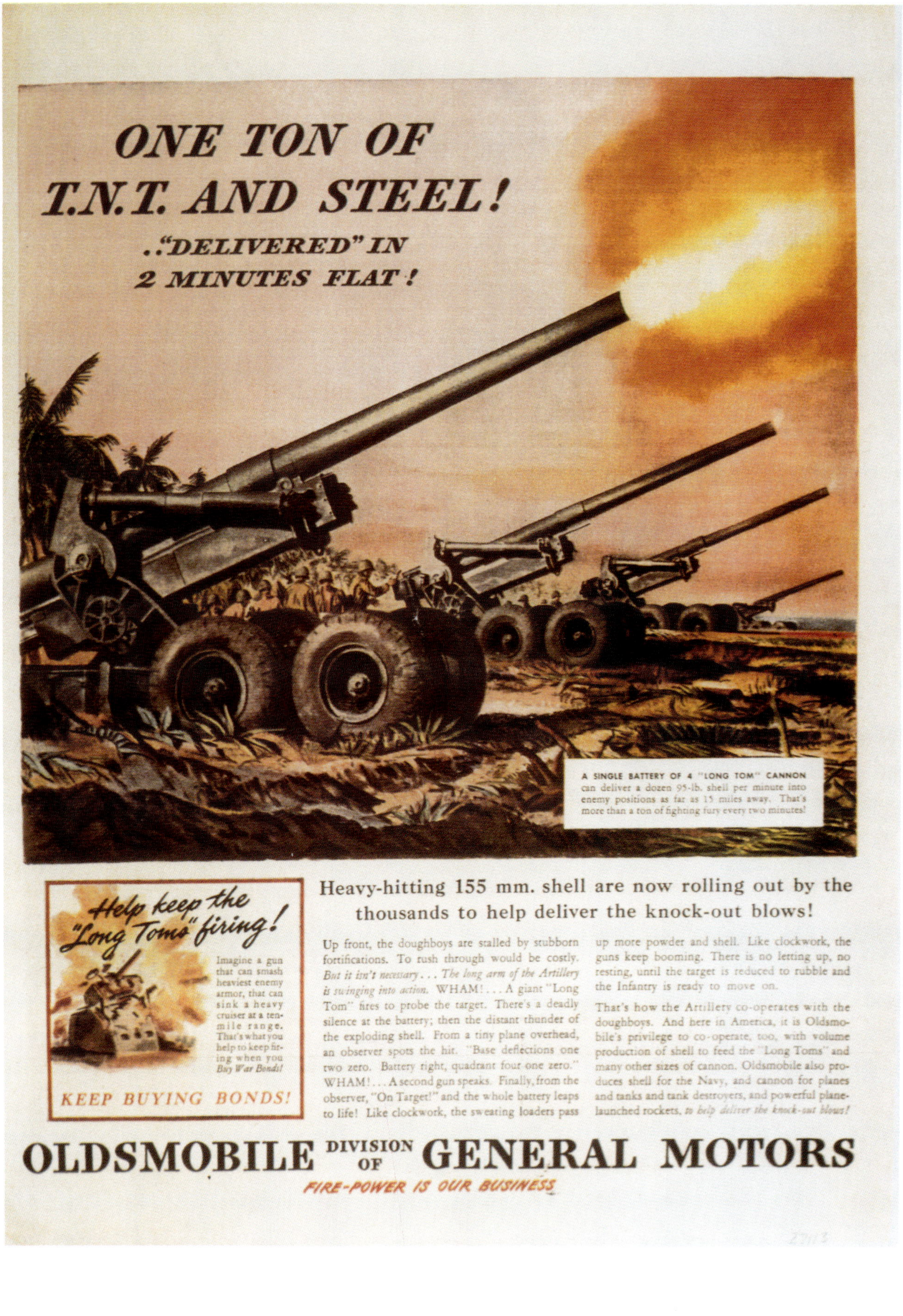
ONE TON OF
T.N.T. AND STEEL!
..."DELIVERED" IN
2 MINUTES FLAT!
A SINGLE BATTERY OF 4 "LONG TOM" CANNON can deliver a dozen 95-lb. shell per minute into enemy positions as far as 15 miles away. That's more than a ton of fighting fury every two minutes!
Help keep the "Long Toms" firing!
Imagine a gun that can smash heaviest enemy armor, that can sink a heavy cruiser at a ten-mile range. That's what you help to keep firing when you Buy War Bonds!
KEEP BUYING BONDS!
Heavy-hitting 155 mm. shell are now rolling out by the thousands to help deliver the knock-out blows!
Up front, the doughboys are stalled by stubborn fortifications. To rush through would be costly. But it isn't necessary... The long arm of the Artillery is swinging into action. WHAM!... A giant "Long Tom" fires to probe the target. There's a deadly silence at the battery; then the distant thunder of the exploding shell. From a tiny plane overhead, an observer spots the hit. "Base deflections one two zero. Battery right, quadrant four one zero." WHAM!... A second gun speaks. Finally, from the observer, "On Target!" and the whole battery leaps to life! Like clockwork, the sweating loaders pass up more powder and shell. Like clockwork, the guns keep booming. There is no letting up, no resting, until the target is reduced to rubble and the Infantry is ready to move on.
That's how the Artillery co-operates with the doughboys. And here in America, it is Oldsmobile's privilege to co-operate, too, with volume production of shell to feed the "Long Toms" and many other sizes of cannon. Oldsmobile also produces shell for the Navy, and cannon for planes and tanks and tank destroyers, and powerful plane-launched rockets, to help deliver the knock-out blows!
OLDSMOBILE DIVISION OF GENERAL MOTORS
FIRE-POWER IS OUR BUSINESS

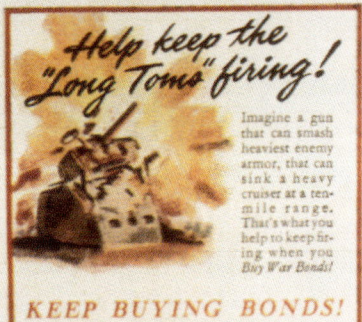

BLACK PANTHER
WITH FISTS FULL O' FIRE!

From out of the blue, as if from nowhere, a formation of "Lightning" fighter planes streaks after the enemy. It's the Black Panther Squadron—America's "84th"—whose fighting insigne is the snarling panther with fists full of fire. True to their battle emblem, the men of the "84th" are daring and skillful fighters. Their planes are among the fastest and highest fliers of all. And at their command is the Fire-Power of long-range, fast-firing, heavy-hitting cannon! Here's a salute to the Black Panthers of the air—with good wishes, good luck, and "good hunting" in every mission against the enemy!

OFFICIAL INSIGNE
OF THE
84TH FIGHTER SQUADRON
U.S. ARMY AIR FORCES

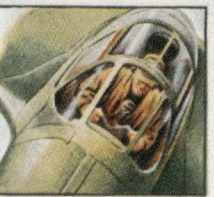

THEY'RE FIGHTING FOR US—AND COUNTING ON US!
Let's not let them down. The closer we get to Victory the tougher the fighting becomes. Now's the time to
Buy War Bonds!

Some of the heroic performances of America's fighter pilots in this war have been so amazing as to be almost unbelievable. There's the group of fliers, for example, who attacked and sank an enemy destroyer with nothing but the Fire-Power of their cannon-firing Lightnings . . . the Air Forces officer who shot down two enemy fighters with only three cannon shell . . . the pilot who exploded enemy locomotives, knocked out enemy tanks, smashed enemy installations—all with cannon Fire-Power . . . Such deeds stand as a fine tribute to the courage, the skill, the all-round fighting ability of the Army Air Forces personnel. We, at Oldsmobile, feel it has been a privilege to build thousands of the cannon these men are using in combat. In addition to *aerial* Fire-Power, we are also building several other types for both Army and Navy . . . cannon for tanks and tank destroyers, shell for tanks, artillery and naval guns. All to "Keep 'em Firing!"

OLDSMOBILE DIVISION OF GENERAL MOTORS
FIRE-POWER IS OUR BUSINESS

World War II

Gun School

World War II

Gun School

In January, 1942 Oldsmobile opened a training school for servicemen instructors. Individuals were trained on repair and maintenance on the various cannon which Olds produced. The school was housed in the Bldg. 64 auditorium. A year later the school would start training servicemen themselves.

Opposite page-A few of training manuals developed during this timeframe.
This page left & center left-This is how the groups travelled to the plant, they walked. **Center right**-A group with a .50 caliber M2 aircraft gun. **Bottom left**-Typical classroom in operation. **Bottom right**-.50 cal gun class in session.

World War II

Gun School

Regular classroom work was required for a variety of parts. **Above left**-20mm cannon classroom. Each room contained the item that the group was being trained on. **Upper right and below**-These men are learning about Pratt and Whitney connecting rods and how the radial engine worked. H. S. McHenry is the instructor.

World War II
Gun School

Sections of an actual aircraft were used to show how the Olds guns were installed. This allowed the students to better understand how maintenance and repairs could be done in the field. J. J. Dobbs, war products training school manager, is in the center of the left photo.

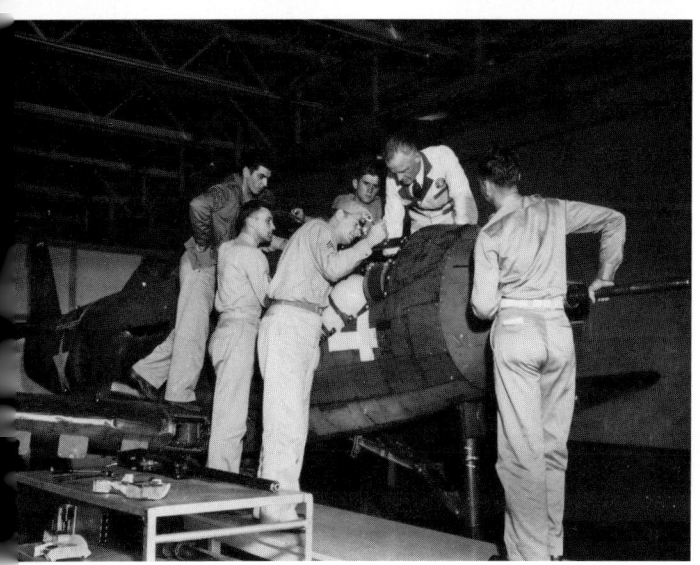

Gun School

World War II

SCHOOL LAYOUT

WAR PRODUCTION – SERVICE DEPARTMENT LAYOUT

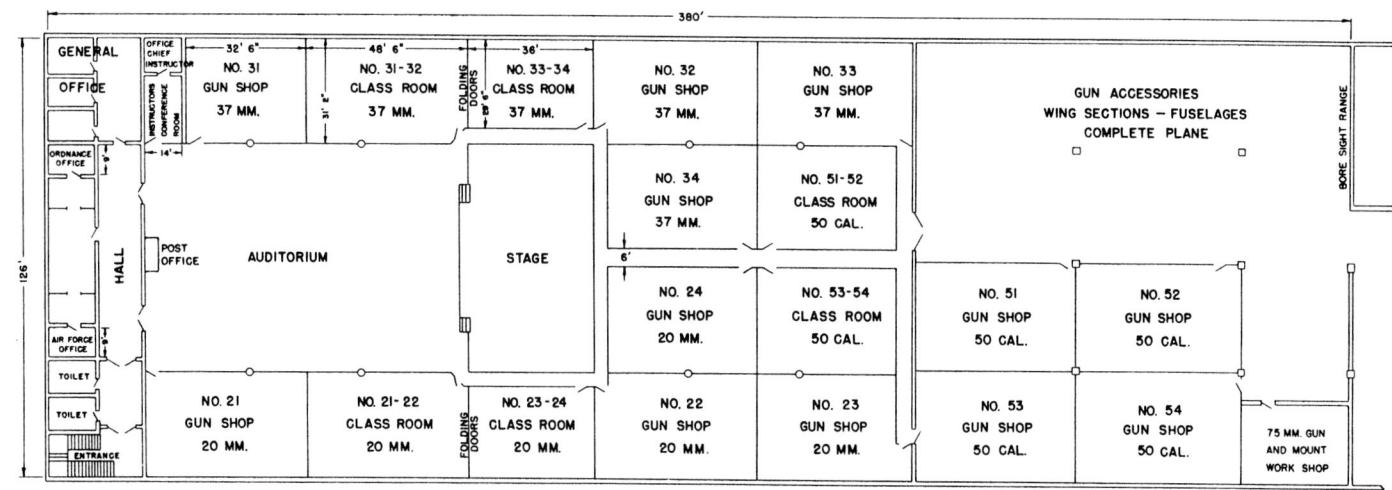

SCHOOL TRAINING FACILITIES

World War II

Gun School

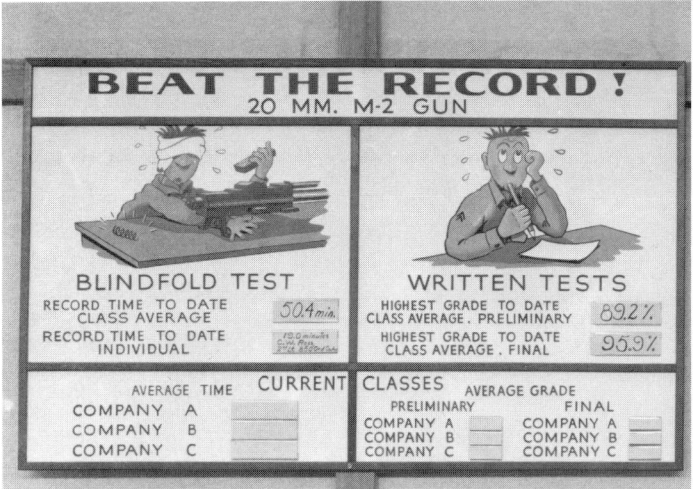

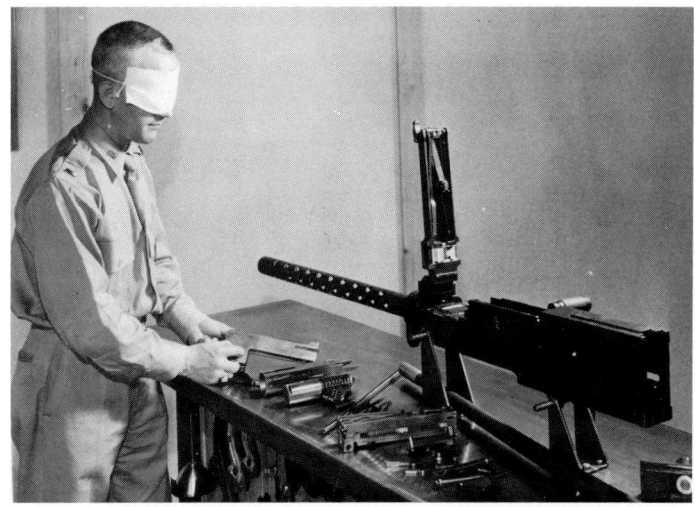

Opposite page top-The gun school layout in Bldg. 64. **Bottom**-The blindfold assembly test. PFC Ed Monoski demonstrates his abilities in front of A. Westman, H. Hidlay of Olds and W. Baker of the U. S. Army. The bullseye flag in back will be discussed later.
This page top left-Blindfold test record times. **Top right**-Blindfold test. **Center and left**-Graduating classes in the auditorium.

World War II

Bond Drives

Bond and fund drives provided the cash to help fund the war effort. Lansing and Oldsmobile did their part. Everyone participated!

Upper right-Helen Hayes, noted actress, on stage at the Olds auditorium in front of the WJIM radio mike in May 1942. **Upper left**-Sidewalk sign in downtown Lansing. **Right**-Downtown banner on Washington Ave. for the Ingham County War Fund Drive. Funds were needed both nationally and locally to support the war effort and to help the needy.

World War II

Bond Drives

Upper left-Enticements like the "Win a Bond" poster here helped to get everyone in the mood. **Upper right**-Olds donated bonds to help in the fund drives. **Left**-Billboard sign for the Ingham County drive.

Bond Drives
World War II

Above-A drawing for one of the bond winners. Note the "V" for victory on the shirt of the man by the barrel. This photo was taken at the Forge Plant. All union members belonged to Local 652 at that time. **Right**-Marjorie Brooks (Schmidt), a plant secretary, models one of the many "T" shirts used during this period.

World War II

Bond Drives

Left-Sherrod Skinner (L) and two other men at a bond rally. **Below**-Harold Moon models another T shirt. **Bottom left**-Bonds were given for winning suggestions. Dorothy Leamy holds two bags of money signifying the $1,000 per month given away. **Bottom right**-Olds received citation, held by Comptroller Earl Schuon, from the U.S. Department of Treasury on January 23, 1943 for effort in the bond drives.

World War II

Bond Drives

In June 1943, Olds developed a "Buy a Bomber" bond drive at the suggestion of Alva McWilliams. The photo below is of the Mitchell B-25 named for Oldsmobile employees. McWilliams (R) is shown in the bottom photo purchasing a bond from Emil Linn to help in the cause.

Oldsmobile Employes' Bomber, Bought with Bonds, Joins U. S. Air Force

World War II
Bond Drives

Above left-Three unidentified men at a bond station. **Above**-Stanley Weber in the bond window sells a bond to Fred Hasbany. **Left**-Bond station in Building 60 lobby. **Below left**-Albert Dykhoff (L) and Rome Perkins look at the status of the bond drive. **Below**-Fred Sanders with the pennies buys a bond from C. Brandel.

World War II
Bond Drives

Initially, achieving bond quotas was easy. As the war wore on it became increasingly difficult to reach the goals set for Olds. By the time the war was nearing the end, the 7th war loan was struggling. The Olds *Cannoneer* expressed concern several times during this period. Signage continued to drum up support. The photos here show a variety of activities used to improve sales.

World War II
Bond Drives

World War II

Entertainment

War work took much of the employees' time. However, other activities helped to make the effort seem less time consuming. Parades in downtown Lansing were held each year. Olds always provided a float as shown **right and below**. **Below right**-Most shopping was done in downtown Lansing, no malls existed. **Bottom left**-The Exhibit and Display Dept. made a good many displays for public and plant viewing. This one was set up in the Olds Auditorium. **Bottom right and opposite page**-Building 60, the Administration Building, was always decorated for the Christmas holidays.

World War II

Entertainment

World War II

Entertainment

General Motors produced a travelling road show that came to Lansing. It was a patriotic musical which played at the Michigan Theater. **This page**-The theater marquee for the December 1943 review. **Opposite page top**-The crowd inside the arcade. Note the gun displays. The shop with the flag banner was the Wings recruiting office (see page 125) **Bottom left**-A family at the review of December 1942. **Bottom right**-The lobby area.

World War II

Entertainment

World War II

Entertainment

The Oldsmobile Quarter Century Club was formed in the '30's to recognize those employees who had achieved 25 years of service. Olds was an old organization by this time, having been born in 1897. Most of the older car companies had gone out of business by this time and Olds was the grandfather of them all. The war effort did not stop the Quarter Century group from inducting additional members into its ranks. **This page**-Bill Mahoney (L) talks to a group of rather happy looking men as he tells one of his typical Irish stories. (L-R) Mahoney, Dick Pollock, Burk Sharp, Fred Seymour and William Bennett. Mahoney was Olds personnel director for many years.

Opposite page top-Sherrod Skinner, general manager (dark suit) and Brig. General A. G. Gillespie commanding officer of the Watervliet Arsenal, sit with a group of women members. (L-R rear) Honoura Hookway, Erma Norton, Rosa Hess, Edith Cushman, (front) Bettye Hemmer, Gillespie, Skinner and Bessie McCree. **Bottom**-Skinner at the podium giving the address for the evening. The service awards for the new 25 year members as well as the updated rings and pins for the longer service individuals are on the display stand in front. This meeting was held in August 1944 at the Hotel Olds.

World War II

Entertainment

115

Entertainment

World War II

The General Motors Girls' Club on their 10th Anniversary presents an Anniversary Dance Saturday March 10th Engineering Auditorium Dancing 9 to 1 with Ed Berry and his Orchestra DOOR PRIZES $1.00 PER PERSON ★ TICKETS LIMITED — GET YOURS EARLY Proceeds to be used for War Activities

World War II

Entertainment

The Engineering Auditorium was the scene of a great many activities during the war. The auditorium portion was kept open even though the gun school used much of the area around it during the early portion of the war. The General Motors Girls club was active in fund raising for the war effort.
Opposite page top-A group of women holds the poster for the 10th anniversary dance held on March 10, 1945 in the auditorium. **Bottom**- Victory gardens to grow vegetables for home use and planting flowers were springtime activities that most people looked forward to. Practically every person had a small space of land planted to something. Helen Fuller ponders what seeds to purchase.
This page-Another auditorium use was a bingo party held in March 1944. The largest party held up to this time, 550 people were in attendance. Funds collected were for the British War Orphans. You will note by this time the gun school had been removed and the whole room was again open for use.

Entertainment

World War II

World War II

Entertainment

Opposite page-Sports activities had always been popular at Olds. This continued during the war. Basketball teams were sponsored for both men and women. The Forge Plant had its own team. **Top**-(L-R) Arnold Harvey, Daryl McElmurry, Ken Gothro, Jim Birney, Jack Waters, Frank Newhouse, Lyle Padgett, R. Hopkins, Rocky Walker, Bob Nisbet and Jack Treanor. **Bottom Left**-(L-R back) Ted Tycocki, Fred Deschow, Frank Boch, Don Barker and Bill Kemp. Front-Roy McLeod, James Long, Willard Powers and Ken Palmer. **Bottom right**-(L-R back) Barbara Ryder, Wilma Barbour, Willene Cline and Hazel Mullett. Front-Phyllis Force and Beverly Skinner.

This page-The plant also sponsored open houses to allow families and friends to view plant operations. Servicemen home on leave also attended and were very popular with the employees. **Below**-(L-R) Jack Henry, Agatha Ahler, Clarence Courtright and Betty Ahler talk to an unidentified employee.

The E Award

"...FOR HIGH ACHIEVEMENT IN THE PRODUCTION OF WAR EQUIPMENT"

World War II

The E Award

On August 10, 1942 Oldsmobile received the covetted Army Navy E Award for excellence in war materiel production. In typical fashion, Olds had a large ceremony in front of the engine plant. The whole factory was invited and from the looks of the photos of the day, most employees must have attended. The E Award was a way the government had to bolster patriotism and instill continued enthusiasm in the employees of companies participating in war work. Companies could further obtain stars on the flag for continued "high achievement" in production. Olds would eventually get three stars for their efforts. Janesville and Kansas City would also receive E flags.

Opposite page-The front of the E Award invitation booklet.

This page top-Col A. B. Quinton, Jr. at the podium. **Bottom right**-Michigan Governor VanWagoner speaks to the audience. **Bottom left**-General Gillespie shares his views with the group.

121

The E Award

World War II

122

World War II

The E Award

Opposite page top-The crowd north of the engine plant watching the presentation. The two light colored buildings in the background are the above ground portion of the gun test range, Building 44. Building 64 is in the far background. **Bottom left**-The Fort Custer band played for the group. **Bottom right**-Sherrod Skinner, Olds general manager (R) and James Bowden, UAW Local 652 Representative (L), talk with members of the presentation delegation. A 75mm cannon barrel can be seen at the bottom of this photo.

This page top left-General Gillespie (L), Bowden and Skinner hold the flag at the luncheon meeting. **Top right**-Charlie Blades, Olds longest service employee, receives his E pin from Geraldine Ahern as Pvt. Joseph Adams from the gun school looks on. **Left**-The E flag flies with Old Glory above Bldg. 60. **Bottom left**-Olds received the first star on February 6, 1943 and the second in October the same year. **Bottom right**-Janesville also received the E flag. Tom Downey (L), Charles Wilson, soldier, Skinner and others make the presentation.

World War II

Women in the Workplace

Women had worked in a variety of Olds production jobs as far back as 1907. The war brought about considerable demand for new employees to replace the men who went into the services. The Olds Wings program was developed to address that need by promoting the idea of the woman in the workplace.

World War II
Women in the Workplace

Opposite page top-Promotional Wings booklet that described working in the factory. **Center and bottom right**-These photos show the uniform with the wing patch that women could wear. **Bottom left**-The wing lapel pin could be worn at events outside the plant.
This page top-The recruiting office in the Michigan Theater Arcade provided a place for women to learn about the program. **Left**-Entering the employment office in the basement of Bldg. 60. **Bottom left**-Getting fitted for safety glasses. **Bottom right**-Passing through the gate.
These photos were designed to make it seem easy for a new woman employee to fit into the industrial atmosphere.

125

Women in the Workplace

World War II

Above-Training session in the classroom on rods. **Right**-Handling breech blocks by fork truck.

Opposite page top-Fitting bushings into rods. **Bottom**-Learning about milling machine work on rods.

World War II

Women in the Workplace

Women in the Workplace World War II

This page-Inspecting shells was a little harder. The parts were considerably heavier than rods. Note the wing patches on the uniforms. The hat was called a "snood." It contained the hair to minimize the chance for intanglement in rotating equipment.

Opposite page top-Machining and inspecting shells. **Bottom**-Spray painting shells. Note the mask that kept paint off the copper rotating band.

World War II

Women in the Workplace

129

Women in the Workplace

World War II

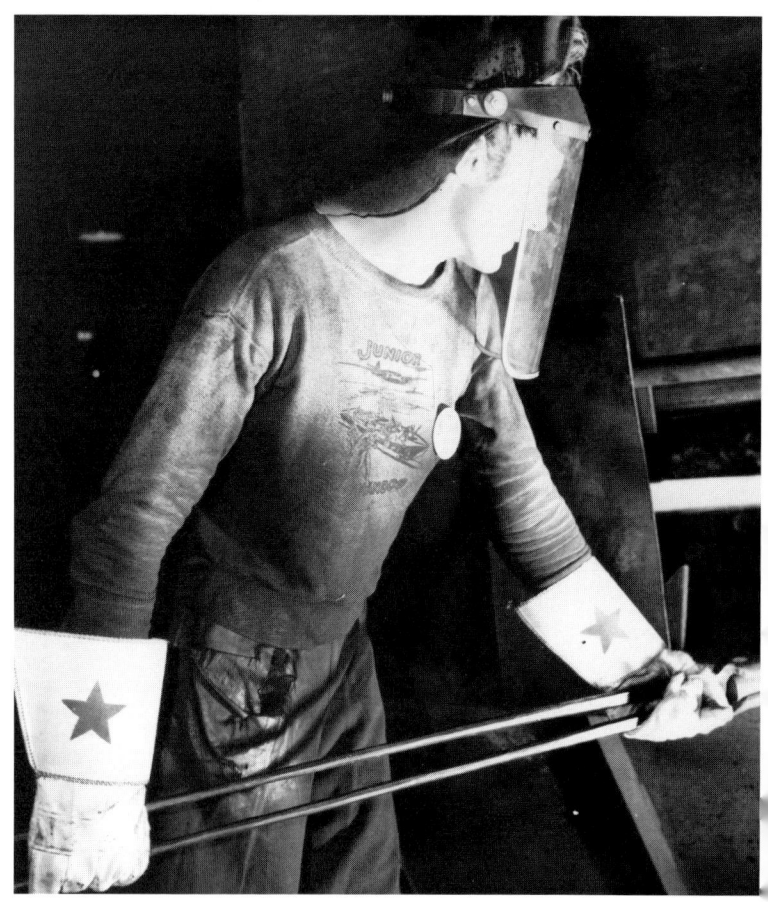

Above-Handling 155mm shells into the shot blast machine. Shot blasting was used to remove forging scale to improve machining capability.
Right-Ruth Amundson is heating forging billets at the forge plant.

World War II
Women in the Workplace

Top left-Preparing boxes for shipping shells from the Forge Plant. **Top right**-Grinding fork rods to remove burrs.
Above-Ruth Shaw (L) and Helen Gardner are handling 75mm cannon tubes on the machining floor.
Left-Women in the office area learning how to use a gas mask.

Visitors
World War II

Oldsmobile had a great variety of visitors during the war period. Many were servicemen returning for leaves or bringing back the word from the front on performance of Olds-made munitions. In many instances Sherrod Skinner would be part of the tour group.

Above-Skinner (R) listens to a serviceman describe part of the 20mm cannon Olds produced. John Dykstra (L) watches. **Right**-Alfred Sloan, GM chairman at the time, paid a visit to the plant in October 1943. Skinner (L) describes a manufacturing operation to Sloan (2nd from left) as Charles Wilson, GM president, and Dykstra look on.

World War II

Visitors

Left-Sloan shakes hands with Chester Hoskins. Hoskins received a $1,000 (the maximum award at the time) for a suggestion he had submitted. **Below**-Donaldson Brown, GM vice chairman; John Dykstra, Olds manufacturing manager; Charles Wilson, GM president; Sloan and Skinner view an operation.

World War II

Visitors

World War II

Visitors

In addition to Alfred Sloan visiting the plant, Ransom Olds was a frequent invitee.
Opposite page top-Sloan touring the 75mm plant. **Bottom**-R. E. Olds (L) smiles as Sloan chats with him. Skinner (R) looks on. **This page top left**-Olds (center) smiles as Skinner (R) shakes hands with an unidentified man. **Top right**-Olds in a Curved Dash. Man is unidentified. **Above**-Olds with great grandson Phillip Bond Fouke III. **Left**-Olds in his office in Olds tower (now Michigan National Tower).

135

World War II
Plant Security

Plant Protection was responsible for maintaining plant security. During the war all officers carried sidearms and were called Auxillary Military Police. **Upper left**-All employees wore a badge like the Floyd Schwab badge. Arms training was carried out at the State Police firing range shown on these two pages. **Right**-Homer Purchis (L) would become chief of Plant Security in later years. **Below**-Division St. gate as it looked from the north in 1943. Gates were manned for both vehicles and pedestrians.

World War II

Plant Security

Top-Firing range. **Center**-The Bldg. 60 Administration Building lobby was guarded by a male receptionist. Here, Dr. H. D. Fong, Chinese educator, signs in. **Bottom**-Parking lot 8 east of the engine plant.

Signage

World War II

At the start of the war, a Keep 'em Firing Committee was formed. The group was made up of both union and management members. One of its purposes was to get everyone on the same team, all pulling together. Much of the plant signage, advertising and printed material originated from this group. **Below**-Oldsmobile's wartime employee publication, the *Cannoneer*, carried this message on the front page of the first issue in January 1942.

World War II

Signage

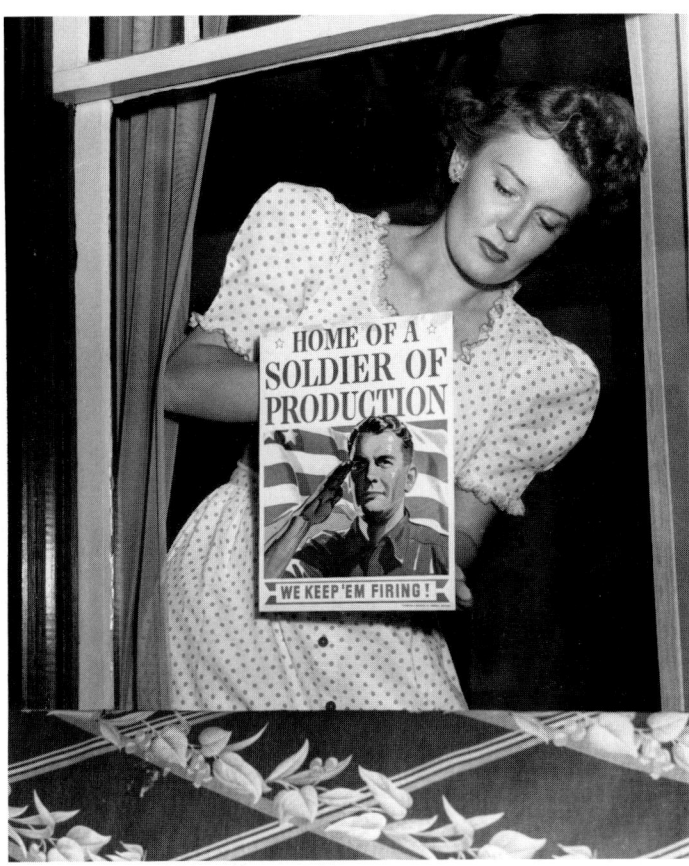

This page top-Home signage was also promoted. **Below**-The KEF (Keep 'em Firing) Committee. (L)R. Roberts, C. Havens, Harold Pohl, Hazen Wilcox, Harold Wilson, George Nader, Theodore Cook and James Bowden. **Bottom right**-In-plant signage was displayed throughtout the manufacturing areas.

OUR BIG JOB AT
OLDSMOBILE-
KEEP 'EM
FIRING!
OLDSMOBILE DIVISION ··· GENERAL MOTORS CORPORATION
CENTRAL ADV. CO.

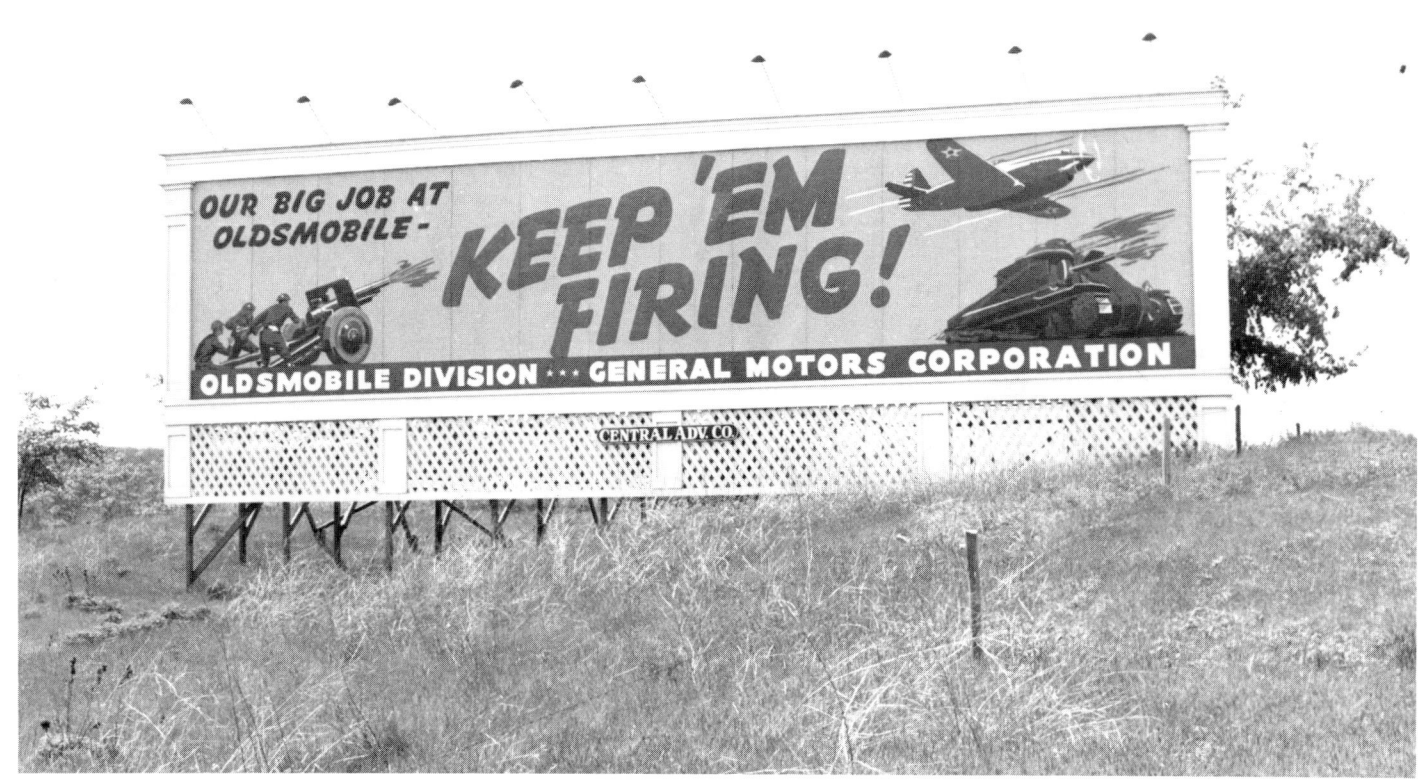

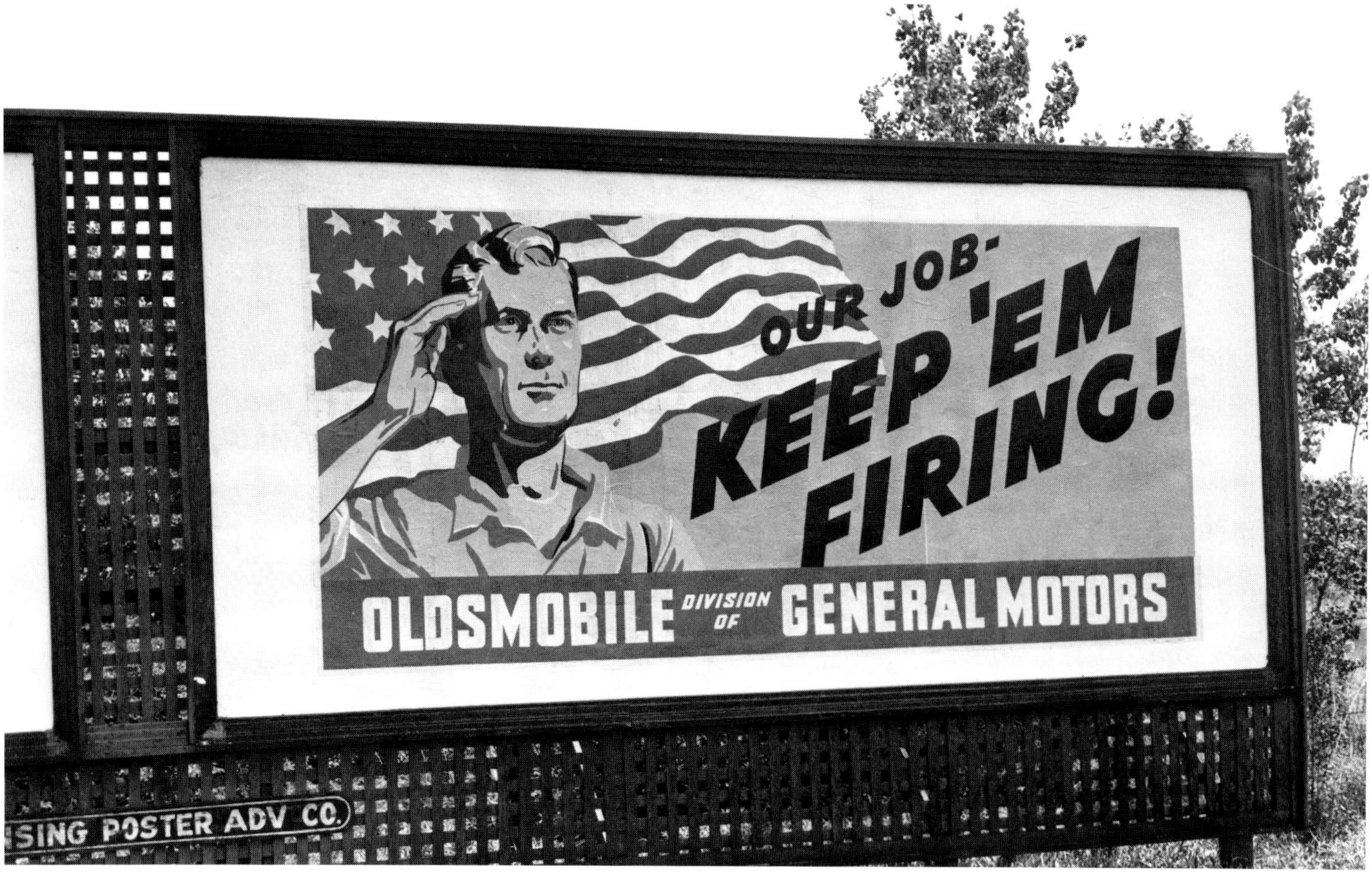
OUR JOB-
KEEP 'EM
FIRING!
OLDSMOBILE DIVISION OF GENERAL MOTORS
SING POSTER ADV CO.

World War II

Signage

Posters and signs could be found everywhere. The roadside signs shown here and on the opposite page were all in the Lansing area. They announced to the incoming vehicles that Olds was in the munitions business. Posters shown below were displayed throughout the plant and changed on a regular basis as part of the effort to keep employees focus on the job of winning the war. Many of the posters were created by outside ad agencies and the government. At Olds, the KEF slogan would be used as a part of the poster.

World War II

Signage

142

World War II

Signage

Most signs portrayed the enemy in a rather unflattering light. Many also played to the natural fears of the employees for their family and country. They were, however, used to keep up the enthusiasm for production of the war materiel we manufactured.

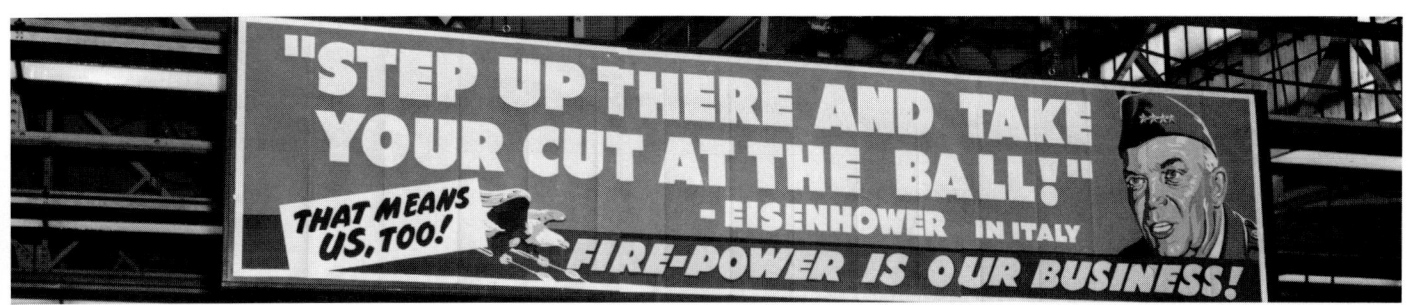

World War II

Signage

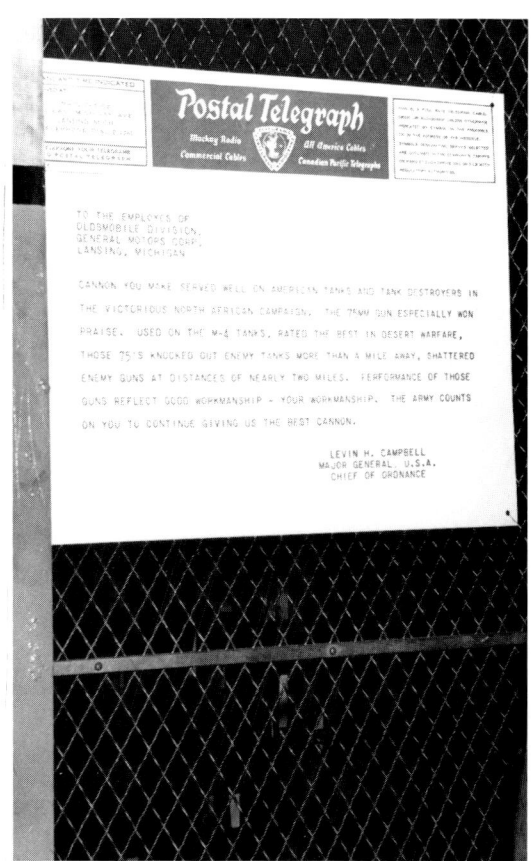

World War II

Signage

Telegrams were received on a regular basis from a variety of service personnel, mostly from the Ordnance Department. You will note one from "Ike" and one from Robert Patterson, undersecretary of war. When telegrams arrived they would be increased in size on heavy yellow paper to simulate real telegrams, and distributed throughout the manufacturing areas. This type of communication with the front did a good job helping the warriers of production maintain their focus and effort.

```
WESTERN UNION

CA492  LG GOVT WAR=WASHINGTON DC MAY 15 1943 NFT
TO THE MEN AND WOMEN OF OLDSMOBILE DIVISION=
       GENERAL MOTORS CORP

THIS MESSAGE FROM THE COMMANDER IN CHIEF OF THE ALLIED
FORCES IN AFRICA IS RELAYED BY THE WAR DEPARTMENT "OUR
FIGHTING MEN, STANDING SHOULDER TO SHOULDER WITH OUR GALLANT
ALLIES, THE BRITISH AND THE FRENCH, HAVE DRIVEN THE ENEMY
OUT OF NORTH AFRICA. IN THIS VICTORY THE MUNITIONS MADE BY
AMERICAN INDUSTRY, LABOR AND MANAGEMENT, PLAYED A VERY
IMPORTANT ROLE. THERE IS GLORY FOR US ALL IN THIS
ACHIEVEMENT"=
       GENERAL EISENHOWER
       COMMANDER IN CHIEF OF THE
       ALLIED FORCES IN AFRICA.
```

```
WESTERN UNION

WU A 13 LG GOVT DETROIT MICH JAN 6 1945 457P
OLDSMOBILE DIVN. S E SKINNER

TO THE MEN AND WOMEN OF OLDSMOBILE:-

YOU ARE PRODUCING PARTS FOR HEAVY ARTILLERY WHICH OUR OVERSEAS
COMMANDERS ARE DEMANDING IN GREATER QUANTITIES IMMEDIATELY. WITHOUT
MORE HEAVY ARTILLERY THE ENEMY MAY BE GIVEN CHANCES TO REST AND
REORGANIZE AND EVEN COUNTERATTACK. THE WAR WILL BE PROLONGED AND
MORE AMERICAN LIVES LOST. TO MEET THIS CRITICAL NEED THE ARMY URGES
AND EXPECTS EACH OF YOU MEN AND WOMEN TO WORK EVERY SCHEDULED WORK
DAY, TO WORK EXTRA HOURS WHEN REQUESTED, TO TAKE NO TIME OFF EXCEPT
WHEN ABSOLUTELY NECESSARY, AND TO HELP RECRUIT AND TRAIN NEW WORKERS
WHEN NEEDED. HAVING LIMITED ALTERNATE SOURCES YOU MEN AND WOMEN
MUST GIVE OUR FIGHTING MEN PARTS FOR MORE HEAVY ARTILLERY SO THAT
THEY CAN BLAST THE ENEMY HARDER THAN EVER BEFORE AND DELIVER THE
KNOCKOUT PUNCHES.
              BRIG. GEN. A. B. QUINTON, JR.
              DISTRICT CHIEF WAR DEPT.
              DETROIT ORDNANCE DISTRICT.
```

```
WESTERN UNION

WU B56 95 GOVT EXTRA  WUX MAY 8 1003A 1945

TO THE EMPLOYEES OF OLDSMOBILE
EVERY AMERICAN WAR WORKER HAD A PART IN OUR GREAT
VICTORY OVER GERMANY. MY HEARTIEST CONGRATULATIONS
TO ALL OF YOU. LET US NOT FORGET, HOWEVER, EVEN ON
THIS JOYOUS OCCASION, THAT WE STILL HAVE AN ENORMOUS
JOB TO DO. THE NATION IS COUNTING ON AMERICAN LABOR
AND INDUSTRY TO PROVIDE THE WEAPONS AND EQUIPMENT
NEEDED TO CRUSH JAPAN. I AM CONFIDENT THAT THIS GREAT
PRODUCTION TEAM WILL DO WHATEVER IS NECESSARY TO SEE
TO IT THAT MILITARY SCHEDULES ARE MET FULLY AND ON TIME.
        ROBERT P. PATTERSON UNDERSECRETARY OF WAR
        WASHINGTON DC
           1208P
```

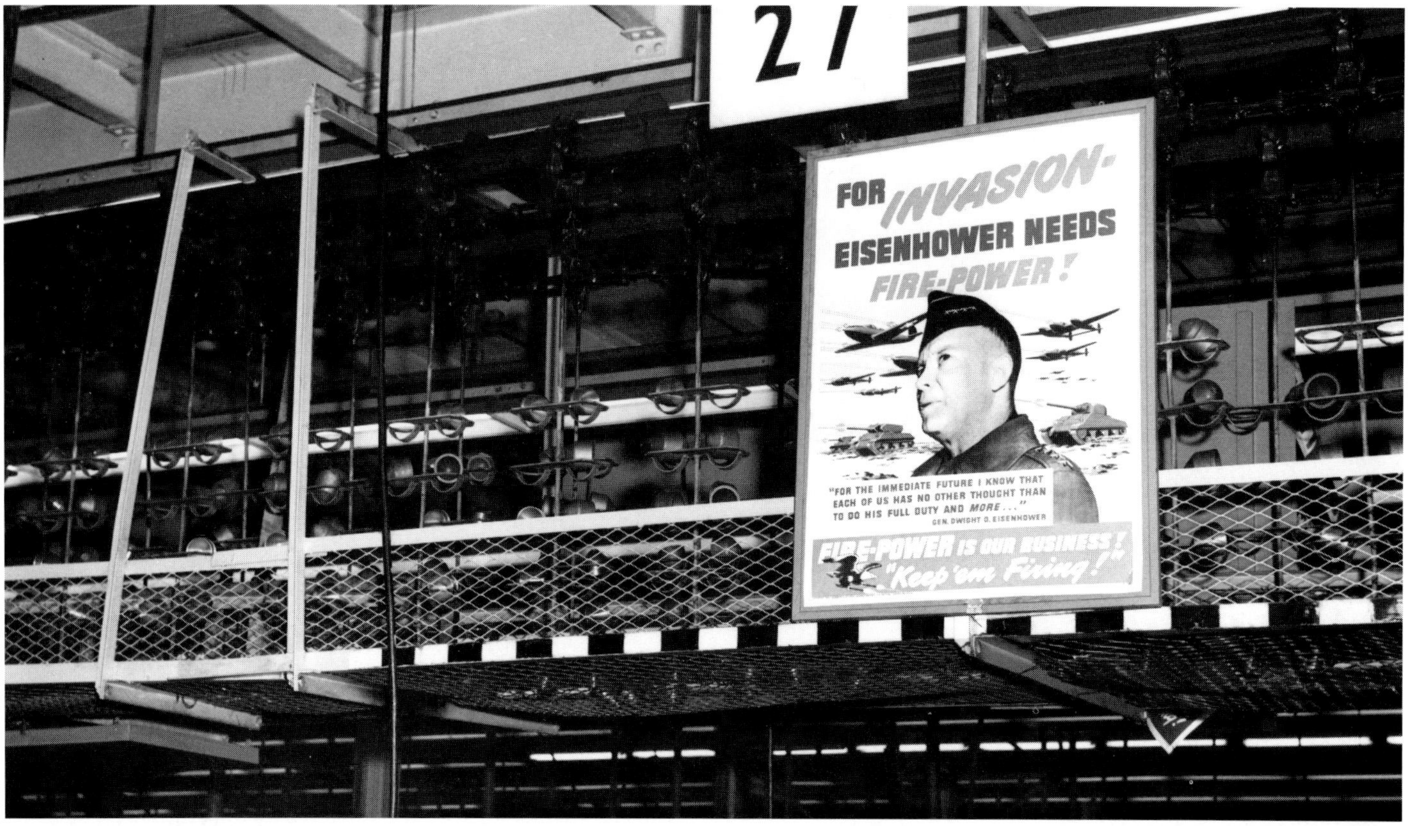
27
FOR INVASION-
EISENHOWER NEEDS
FIRE-POWER!
"FOR THE IMMEDIATE FUTURE I KNOW THAT
EACH OF US HAS NO OTHER THOUGHT THAN
TO DO HIS FULL DUTY AND MORE . . ."
GEN. DWIGHT D. EISENHOWER
FIRE-POWER IS OUR BUSINESS!
"Keep 'em Firing!"

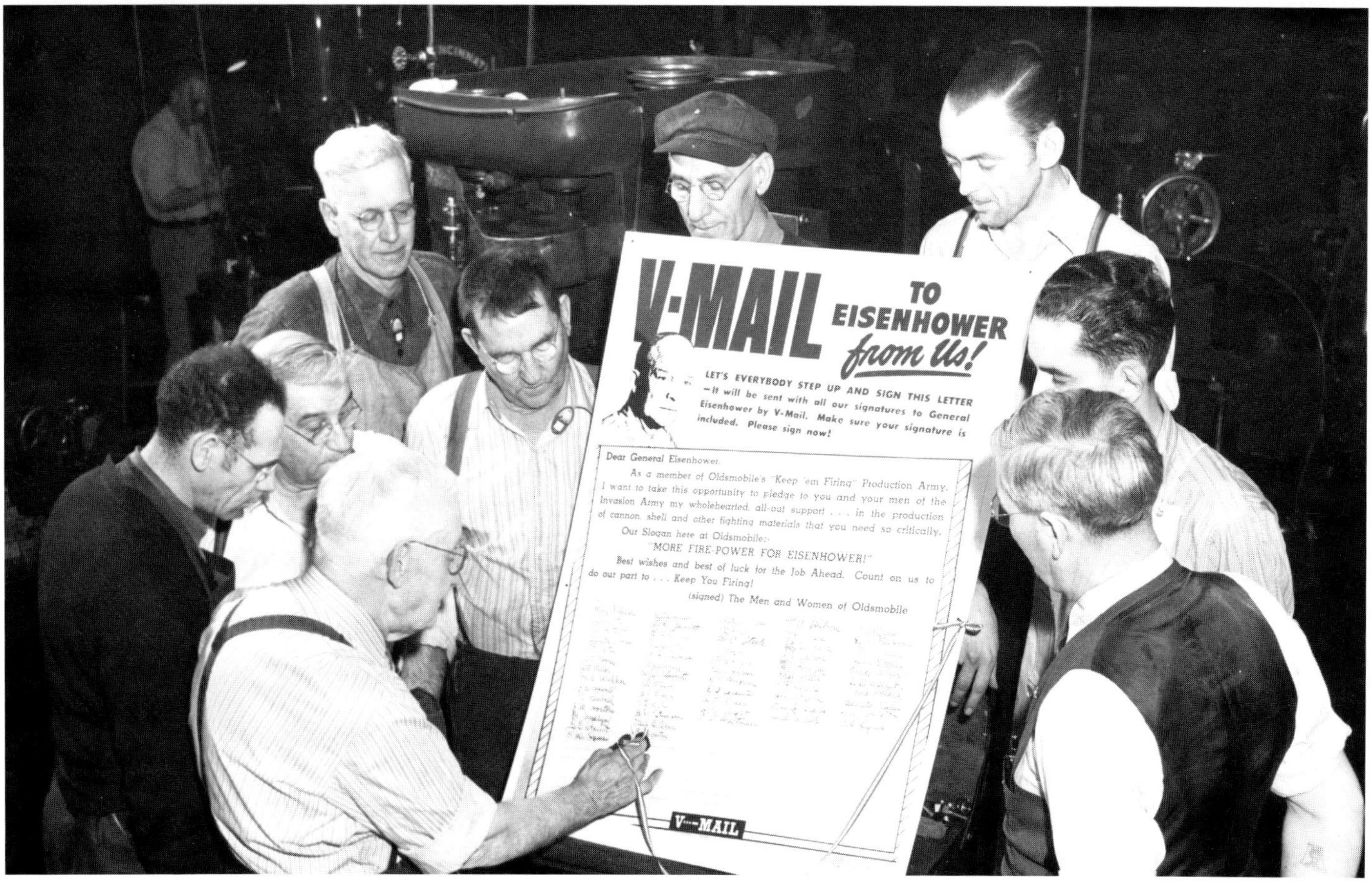
V-MAIL
TO
EISENHOWER
from Us!
LET'S EVERYBODY STEP UP AND SIGN THIS LETTER
—It will be sent with all our signatures to General
Eisenhower by V-Mail. Make sure your signature is
included. Please sign now!
Dear General Eisenhower.
As a member of Oldsmobile's "Keep 'em Firing" Production Army, I want to take this opportunity to pledge to you and your men of the Invasion Army my wholehearted, all-out support . . . in the production of cannon, shell and other fighting materials that you need so critically.
Our Slogan here at Oldsmobile:-
"MORE FIRE-POWER FOR EISENHOWER!"
Best wishes and best of luck for the Job Ahead. Count on us to do our part to . . . Keep You Firing!
(signed) The Men and Women of Oldsmobile
V-MAIL

World War II

Signage

In addition to military type posters, other subjects were covered. From safety to fitness, all subjects were fair game for the poster.

The two photos on the **opposite page** are related to General Eisenhower. Employees and people in general liked Eisenhower and respected his efforts in the war. He was a very popular man. This may also help explain why he was later elected president.

World War II

Signage

Other plant posters. They were located from the tool room to the office as you can see from the photos on these pages.

World War II

Signage

Signage

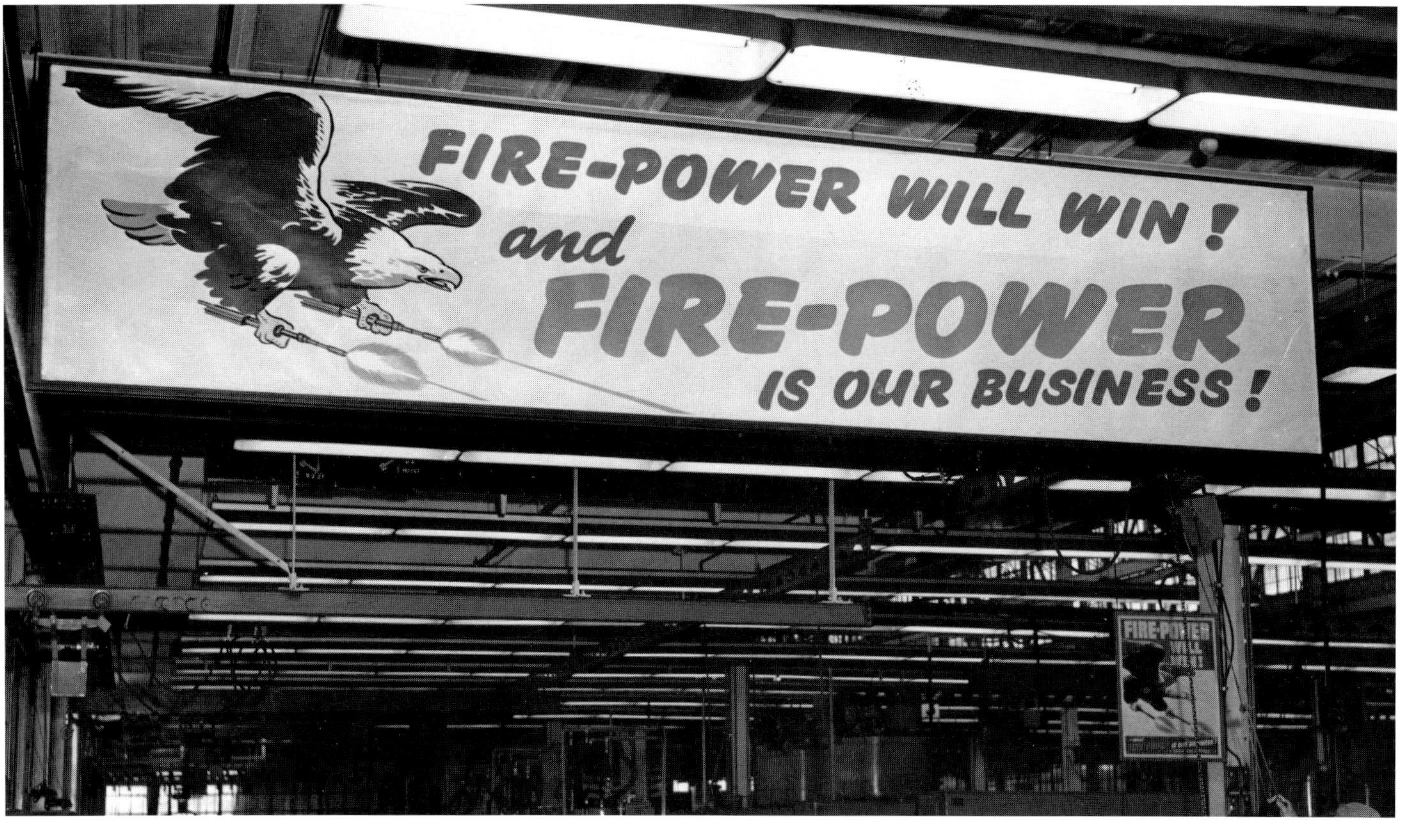

World War II

Signage

Large banners like these shown here were used throughout the plant. The news station **(below)** is typical of those used to provide up-to-date news from the front. WJIM supplied the material received from the wire services. **Bottom-** This large display went to Washington to show the Capitol how things were done in Lansing.

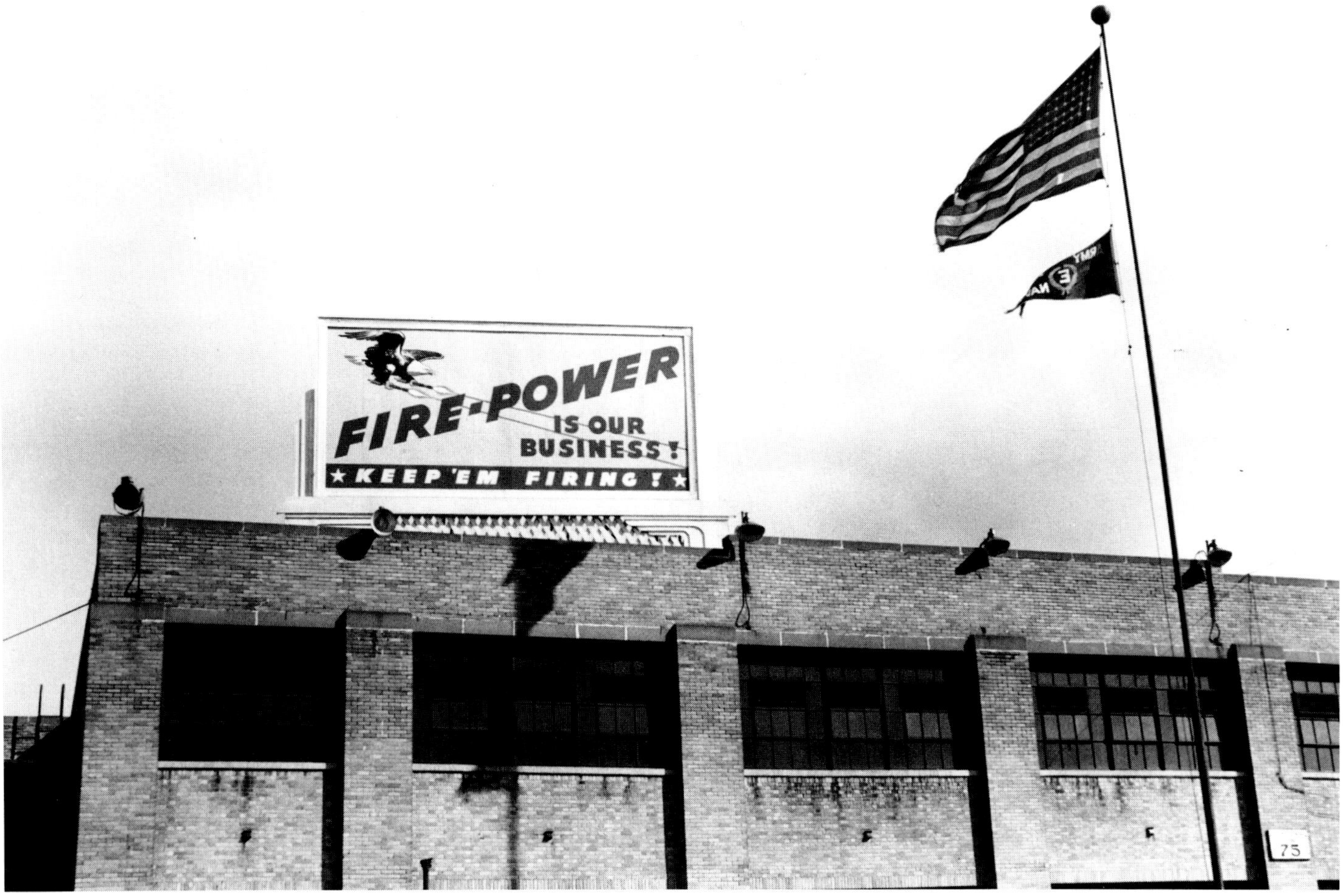

World War II

Signage

World War II

Signage

Opposite page-Additional billboards were used on various plant buildings. **Top**-Building 75 hosted this sign and the American and E flags. **Bottom**-Building 44, the gun test, had these signs on the east wall. Note the American and E flags in front of Bldgs. 36-38 in the background.

This page left-The two Roll of Honor displays are from October 1942 and March of 1943. These hung in the Bldg. 60 lobby. **Below**-In September 1943 there were 1,732 employees in the armed services. Sign outside the safety store in Bldg. 40. By war's end, 2,255 employes served and 52 died. **Bottom**-After VE day in May 1945, we still had to take care of the Pacific war. This poster reminded employees that we were not yet done.

World War II

Other Activities

Right-Tri-City Olds of Miami, FL has a "Keep 'em Rolling" stamp on its stationery. **Below**-If a car needed tires, recaps were available for good carcasses. **Bottom**-Scrap drives were ongoing. The war effort needed tons of raw materials. Even the dealerships participated. Here Whitney Olds has a paper scrap drive.

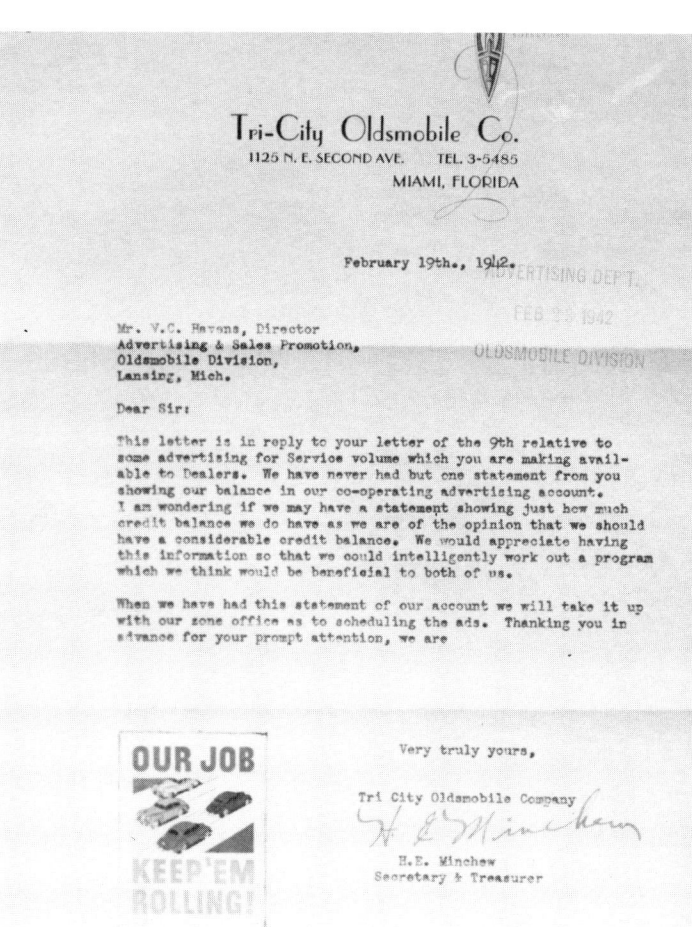

World War II

Other Activities

Below-Scrapping a die in one of the scrap drives. Fortunately, Olds was able to save its antique car fleet from the scrap heap. **Left**-Even Lt. Byron Abbott's scrap keys were worth saving. **Bottom left**-UAW representative Bowden, Lt. General Somervell and Sherrod Skinner in the gun plant. **Bottom right**-D. Standish with his son Clifford, who was home on leave from the Navy.

World War II

Other Activities

World War II

Other Activities

Opposite page-The building 33 and building 40 second floor cafeterias. The 40 cafeteria was located in the north portion of the building and serviced much of the center of the plant. **Top**-(L)Walter Carter, William Bunce and Leroy Sherman. Note the "V" for victory on the caps. **Bottom left**-(L)R. Myers, A. Brandel, F. Murphy and R. Griffin from the management ranks also ate in Bldg. 33.

This page left-The JC's war effort was saving clothes for the Russians. Olds employees helped. Shown here are (L-R back row) Estol Culp, Lyle Padgett, Kenneth McKane, (front row) Warren Bissell, Delos Bauerle, Revell Hopkins, Chairman William Earley and Elmer Ver Merris. **Below**-Olds suppliers were rewarded for good performance just as Olds was with their E flag. This group is receiving the subcontractors' bullseye flag.

157

World War II

Other Activities

This page top left-(L)Sam Crawford, George Barlow, John Wiles and Clarence Fish in the safety store in Bldg. 40. **Right**-A group of twins: co-author Helen Jones (Earley), Bernice Bennett (Jones), Roy Niblick, Ray Niblick, Sharon Laverty and Linda Laverty pose with an aircraft in the gun training school. The Niblicks were student soldiers. The others were Olds employees. **Bottom**-The Olds firewagon was a trailer pulled behind a GMC panel truck.

Opposite page top-Red Cross donation table in Building 60 lobby manned by Jeanette Wilkins, Sales secretary. The offices shown in the back were above the executive garage. This area was originally a vehicle showroom with a turntable. **Bottom**-Felicitas Saier (White) is seated at the table.

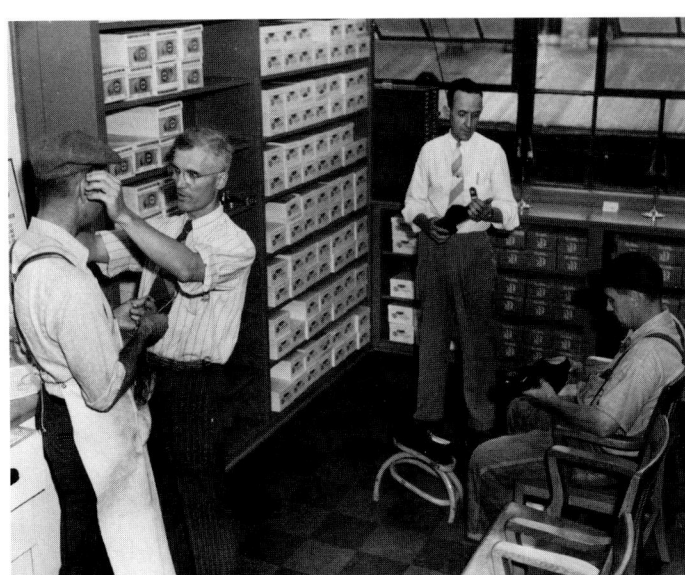

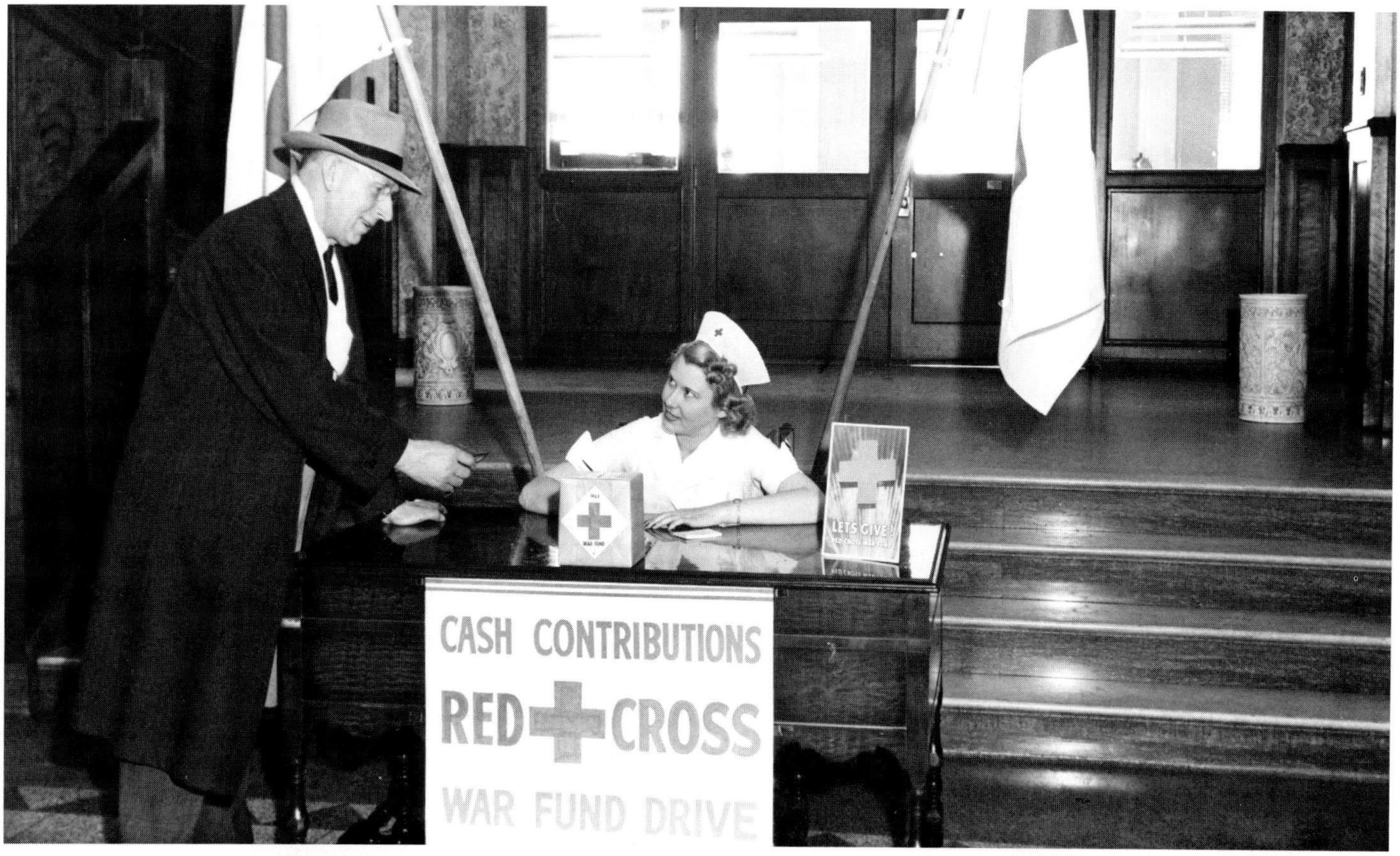

World War II
Other Activities

159

World War II

The Forge Flagpole

The Forge Plant flag pole was dedicated on April 15, 1945 to the 516 Olds men who served and to the ten who gave their lives for the cause. Located east of Building 207, employees and members of the military all were present at the ceremony. Several speakers shared their views with the crowd. **Opposite page bottom**-C. B. Dakin, plant manager, speaking.

World War II

The Forge Flagpole

World War II
Forge Plant Construction

World War II

Forge Plant Construction

Early 1944 Forge Plant construction. **Opposite page**-Digging foundations for Bldg. 207. Bldg. 203, the hammer shop, is in the background.
This page top left-Bridge steel. **Above**-Bldg. 208 brickwork. **Left**-Bldg. 207 steel partially up. This would become the new hammershop. **Below**-Bldgs. 208, 207 & 206 steel as it looked from across Saginaw St., with a muddy mess in the foreground.

World War II
Forge Plant Construction

164

World War II

The War Ends

Opposite page-Buildings 207 and 206 were not immune from signs even though they were being built. These indicate the urgency of the situation in April 1944.

However, the war was nearing an end by spring 1945. **This page top**-Machinery started to move out to make room for car production again. Some shell and gun contracts had been completed by this time. **Bottom**-Training began on what was called "combined operations." This allowed us to get a head start in many areas of the plant.

165

World War II

The War Ends

World War II

The War Ends

Opposite page top-Bldg. 34 dock was used for packing and crating departing machinery. **Bottom**-All equipment was painted in a rust preventative called Cosmoline. It was a mess.
This page top left-Machinery outside of Bldg. 34 dock. **Right**-Elm Street north of Buildings 40 and 34. Pine Street gate is located in the center of the photo by the billboard. Note the raised gatehouse for security purposes. **Bottom**-Elm Street north of Bldgs. 33 and 36. Bldg. 44, the gun test range, is located at the right center of the photo. The two light buildings housed the above ground portion.

Chapter 3 The Korean War

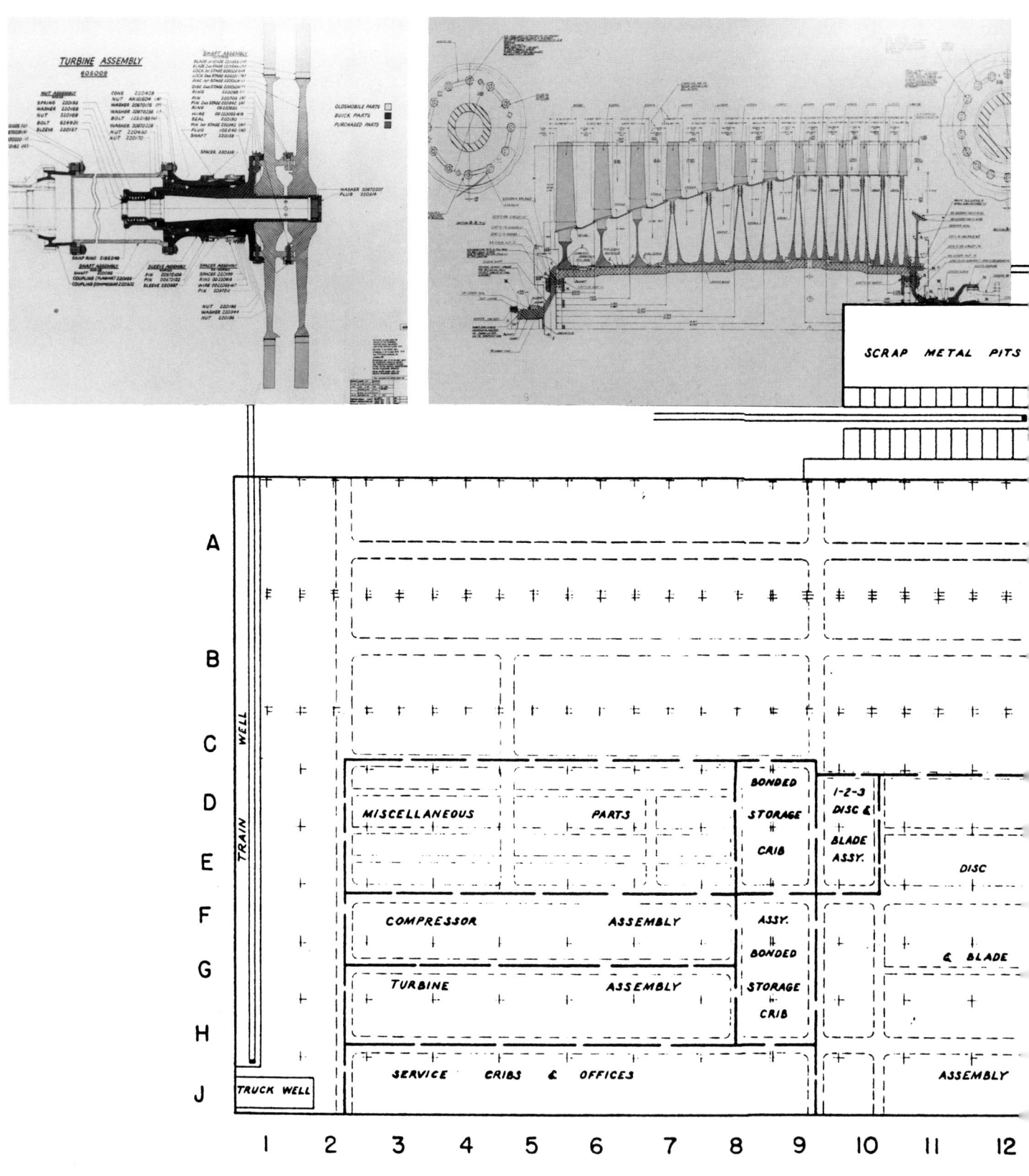

The Korean War

Jet Plant

The Korean War began on June 25, 1950 and ended July 27, 1953. Olds was again called upon to participate in the manufacture of war materiel. The "Jet Job" became a massive undertaking. Land north of the Forge Plant had been purchased for a GM foundry during WWII. It was perfect for the new Jet Plant. In July 1951 construction was started. Products made were the rotating members for the Wright J-65 jet engine. **Opposite page top left**-The turbine was made up of two discs of blades. **Right**-The compressor with 13 discs.

Shown is the Jet Plant layout drawing with locations for the various departments. Assembly is located at the left (north) end of the plant.

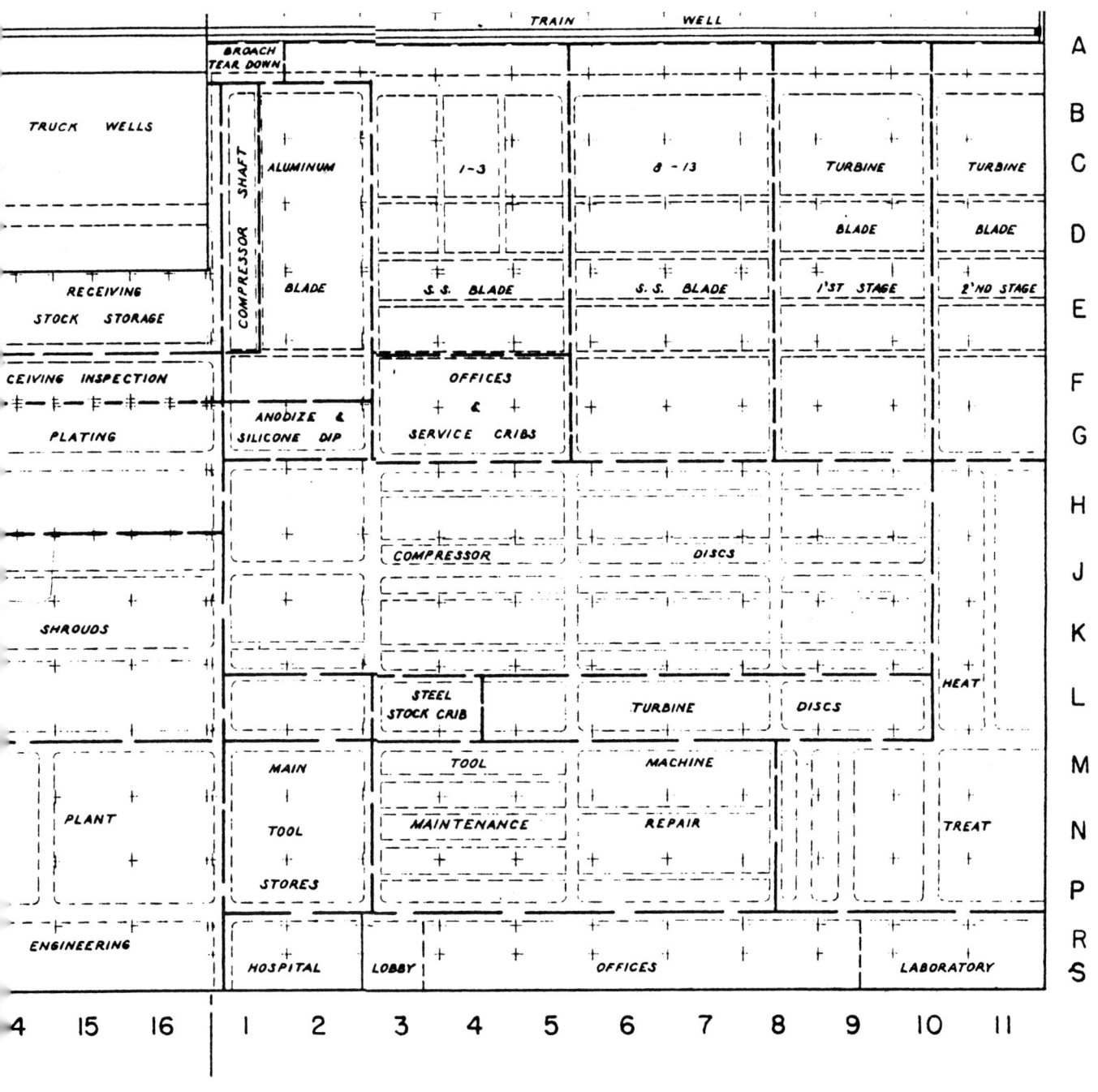

BLDG 302

The Korean War

Jet Plant

170

The Korean War

Jet Plant

Opposite page top-Ground breaking found considerable poor soil. Note the neighbors visiting.
Bottom-Foundations, with three engineers looking on, W. Szpara (L).
This page top-Steel going up in December 1951.
Left-Tossing hot rivets to the man on the steel.
Below-The completed plant in the spring 1952.

The Korean War

Jet Plant

This page-Machining the blades for the jet engine was a different task than we were used to. Specialized blade turners from Pratt and Whitney were required-shown in the **right center and bottom** photos. **Below**-The blade floor with P & W turners on both sides.
Opposite page top-Fitting the blades to a disc. This machine spaced and angled the blades correctly for installation into a disc.
Bottom-Del McRae (L), now general superintendent for the Jet Plant; an unidentified man; Jack Wolfram, general manager; and Don Burnham, manufacturing manager, view a completed disc assembly.

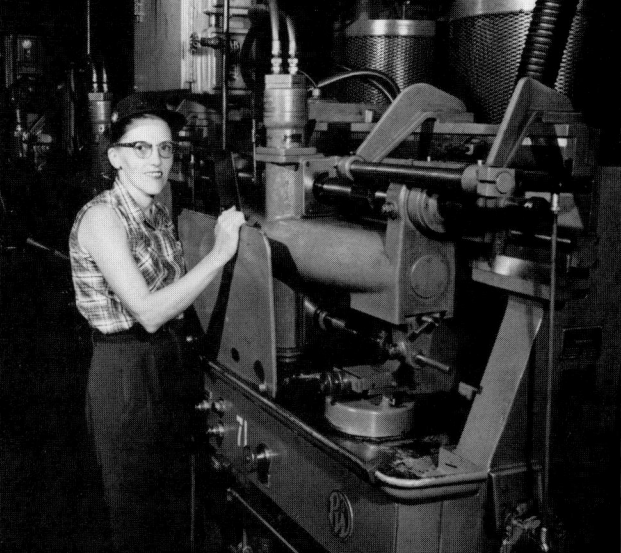

The Korean War

Jet Plant

The Korean War

Jet Plant

The Korean War

Jet Plant

Opposite page top-Turbine discs on assembly cart. **Bottom left**-Turbine assembly ready for assembly to main shaft. **Bottom right**-Grinding machine.
This page top-Compressor assemblies. **Below**-Aligning discs for assembly. **Left**-Completely aligned disc pack ready for assembly.

Jet Plant

This page top-The Olds-designed assembly machine. The shaft is cold and frost coated in preparation for pushing heated discs onto it. This process was developed to speed the assembly operation. Previously, discs were assembled one at a time by forcing them onto the shaft.

Bottom-The assembly machine in operation. **Opposite page top**-A completed compressor assembly in a rollover fixture. **Bottom left**-Assembly in checking gage. **Bottom right**-Assembly cart on track. Carts were hand pushed from station to station.

The Korean War

Jet Plant

The Korean War

Jet Plant

The Korean War

Jet Plant

Opposite page-Rotor test area. Each rotor was spin tested in the covered chamber in the floor. The rotor was driven by a small steam turbine mounted on top. **Top**-Shows chamber in closed condition. **Bottom**-L. Riebow readies a compressor assembly from the rolling rack in back for insertion into test chamber.

This page top-Two disc shaft ready for test. **Bottom**-Del McRae (standing) and Bob Scott, assembly superintendent, look at a completed turbine compressor assembly. Scott pointed out that we never had a rotor explode in the test chamber.

The Korean War

Rockets

The old six cylinder engine plant, Building 28, was used for 3.5" bazooka rocket manufacturing. Production began in late 1951. Millions of bazooka rockets were made in this facility. **Below**-Sherrod Skinner and Jack Wolfram hold one of the rockets. **Opposite page top**-Turning motor bodies on a lathe. **Bottom**-(L-R) Tom Downey, works manager; Jack Wolfram, general manager; S. E. Skinner, general manager accessory divisions; Charles Wilson, GM president; and Don Burnham look at a rocket motor tube during a corporation visit.

The Korean War

Rockets

Rockets

This page top-Forming motor bodies on a press. **Bottom left**-Motor body hydrostatic test. This assured the motor could take the pressure of firing the rocket. **Bottom right**-Loading motor bodies into coating machine.

Opposite page top left-Coating machine. **Right**-Forming nose cones. **Bottom**-Motor bodies being dried by infrared lights.

The Korean War

Rockets

183

Rockets

This page top-Nose cone leak testing fixture. **Bottom**-Nose cone quality control check for dimensions.

Opposite page top-Painting nose cones in an automatic spray booth. Note the belt near the bottom that rotated the cone during the painting process. **Bottom left**-Extension nozzle quality control station. The extension nozzle was the back end of the rocket motor. Extensive quality control was performed throughout the process to assure accurate parts. **Bottom right**-A variety of tail parts were plated in this machine.

TY CONTROL SAMP
STATION
OLDSMOBILE
QUALITY CONTROL

SAFETY
SHOWER

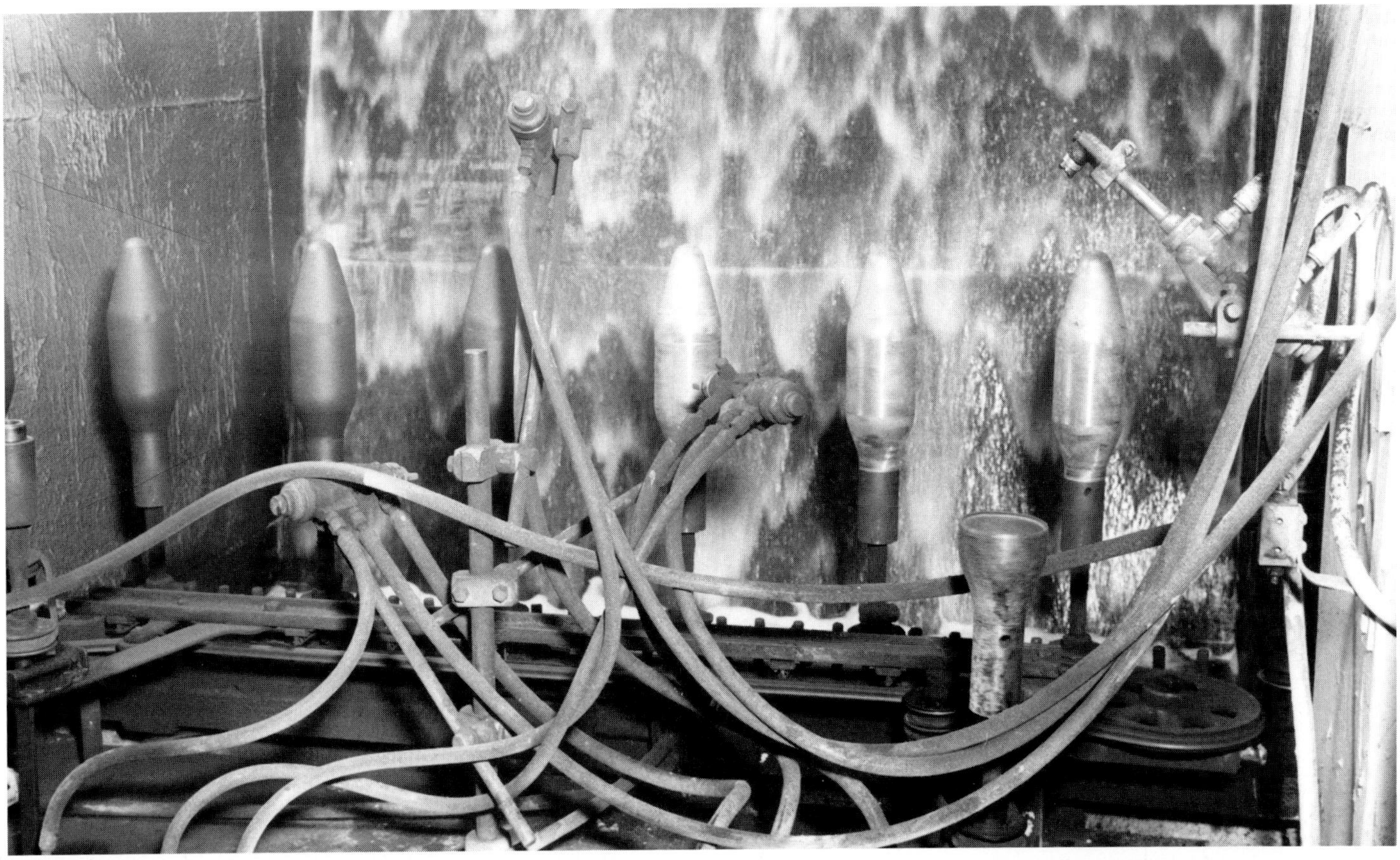

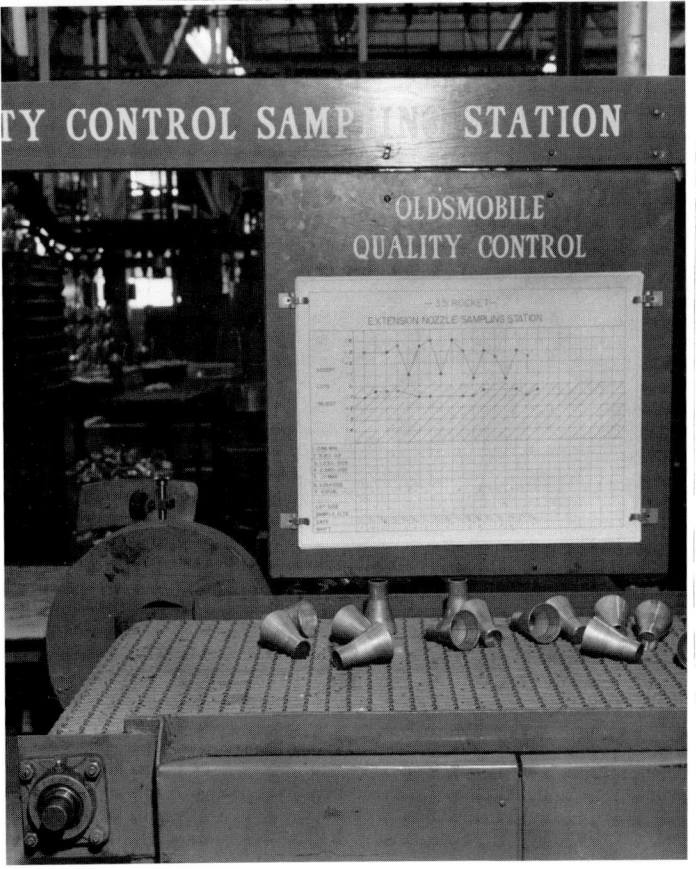

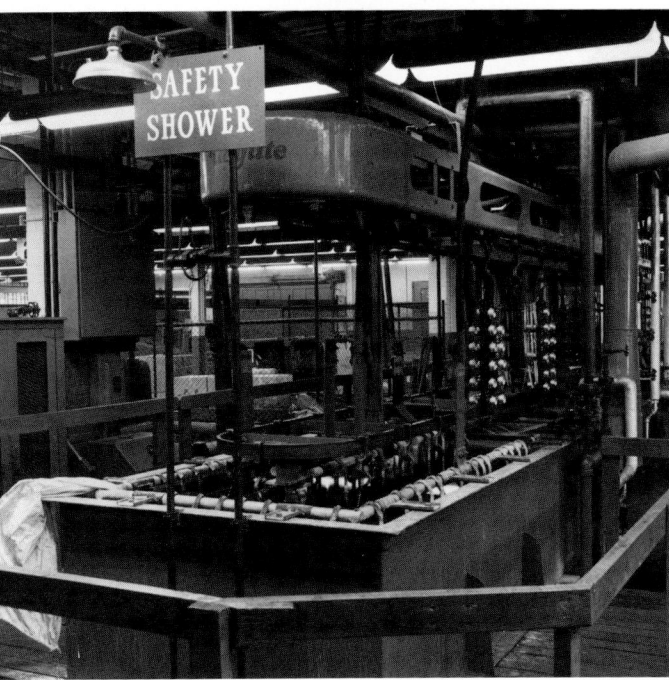

The Korean War

Rockets

Right-Stamping traps. **Below**-Gage for checking traps. **Below right**-Shot blast machine for cleaning traps. **Bottom**-Trap and spacer assembly machine. Traps were part of the nozzle and separated internal motor parts.

The Korean War

Rockets

Above-Tail fin assembly area. Left-Tail spot welding machine. Below-Tail inspection area. Electrical connections in the tail fired the rocket. These had to be checked.

The Korean War

Rockets

This page right-Checking tail assemblies and the igniter connections. **Below**-Painting the motor and tail assembly. **Bottom**-Masking the tail assembly for painting.
Opposite page top-Motor and tail paint drying oven. **Bottom**-Final inspection for the motor assembly.

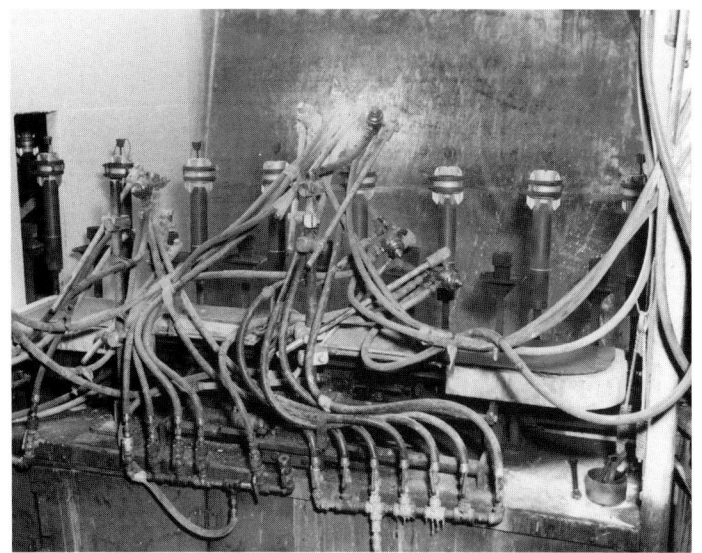

The Korean War

Rockets

The Korean War

90mm Cannon

The Korean War

90mm Cannon

90mm gun production began on January 24, 1951. We manufactured the barrel, breech ring and the breech block and assembled the parts. Building 37 had just been started. This building was planned to be a maintenance and storage building. However, it became our cannon plant.
Opposite page top-Building 37 steel on January 4, 1951. **Bottom**-It wasn't long after the roof started that machinery began arriving. Note the open walls and roof in this photo.
This page top left-(L-R)Jack Wolfram, Jim Edwards, production engineering and methods supervisor, Tom Downey and Don Burnham at the gun model boards for a promotional movie. **Right**-Turning a barrel. **Bottom**-The gun plant looking north in Bldg. 37.

The Korean War

90mm Cannon

Del McRae, gun plant superintendent, is shown in a variety of these photos. His assignment here preceded the Jet Plant program.
This page right-McRae with a lathe operator looking at the turning tooling. **Bottom**-Turning the big end of the barrel.
Opposite page top-Operator hoisting barrel out of a lathe. **Bottom**-Gun assembly with McRae (L) and a group of men. Arnold Hansen, 90mm assistant supintendent, is second from the right. Assembly was in the Bldg. 37 east high bay.

The Korean War

90mm Cannon

The Korean War

90mm Cannon

Charles Wilson, GM president, touring the gun plant. **This page top right**-(L-R) in shadow, Burnham, Harold Metzel, stern Jack Wolfram, Wilson, Skinner, ? and Tom Downey at right. **Top Left**-Burnham, Wilson, operator, McRae in back and Downey with hat. **Bottom**-Skinner, Burnham, Wilson, Downey and Wolfram at the plating machine.

Opposite page top-McRae at operator's position with Downey (R), Griffin behind, Wolfram and two unidentified men. **Bottom**-McRae with hand on gun and a group at gun assembly.

The Korean War

90mm Cannon

90mm Cannon

This page top-Barrel straightening took a large hydraulic press. It was also quite impressive to watch the bend necessary to straighten a tube. **Bottom**-Checking the cannon bore.

Opposite page top-The end of the assembly line. The banks of lights were for drying the paint. **Bottom**-Another tour group views the breech end of a gun. The operator holds a shell casing.

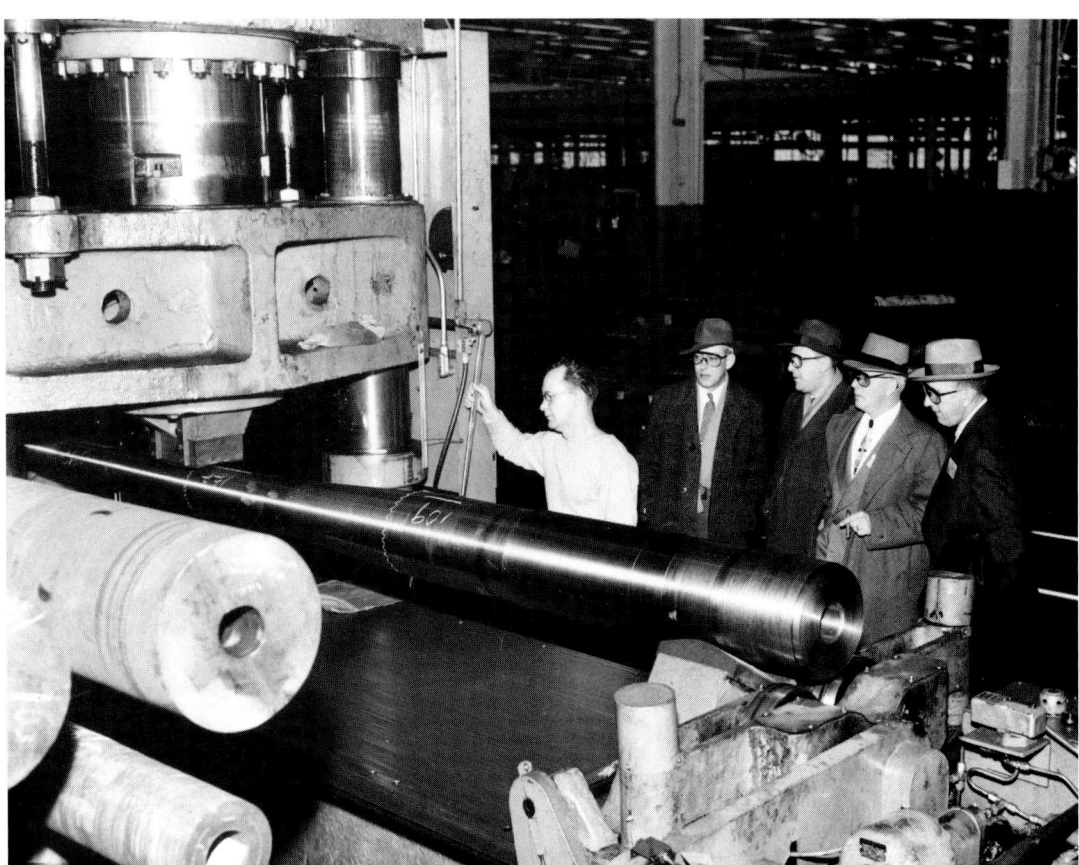

The Korean War

90mm Cannon

90mm Cannon

This page top-Breech rings were large and heavy. They were about a foot cube and almost solid. **Bottom**-Rings arrived at the plant in railroad cars. The side track went right into Bldg. 37 for their removal.

Opposite page top-Machining the ring. This work was done in the east low bays of Bldg. 37 where old Bldg. 34 dock used to be. **Bottom**-The gun program ended in 1954. Here the large lathes are being prepared for shipping to the Government warehouse for storage.

The Korean War

90mm Cannon

The Korean War

MacArthur Visit

General Douglas MacArthur visited the plant on May 15, 1952. His tour took him through all the war production areas and throughout the plant. **This page top**-MacArthur shakes the hand of Forge employee Howard Hale. Hale was in the Pacific war with MacArthur. Charles Glass(R) and Maynard Cornell (L) watch. **Bottom**-MacArthur (center) is surrounded by other visitors and GM brass.

Opposite page top-Much of the visit was by tour train. Monty Childs was the train driver with GM President Charles Wilson and MacArthur in the front of the first coach.
Bottom-Olds also made a few of these 30mm cannon. The gun is shown in a test cell off site (perhaps at the Proving Grounds). Work began with a contract for six guns and development work in November 1951. Production work was done in the Product Engineeering facilities.

The Korean War

Other Guns

Chapter 4 Later Activities

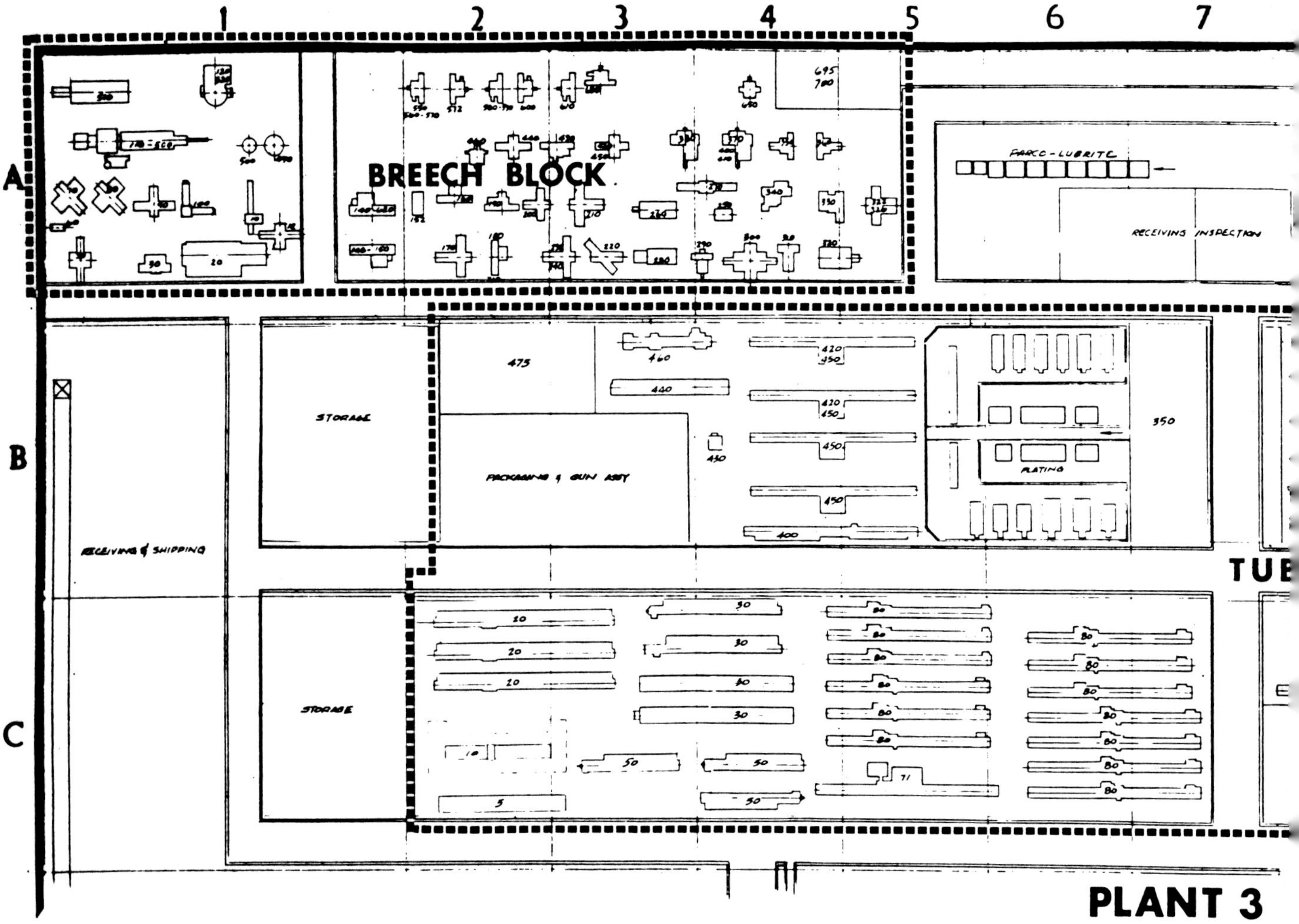

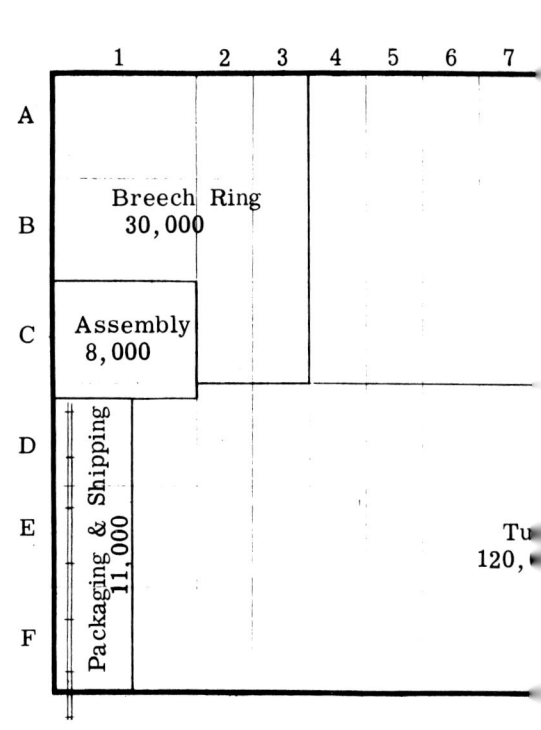

Following the Korean War and the subsequent removal of the machinery for making the various products, Olds continued to be classified as a supplier for cannon and rockets. By the time 1955 rolled around we were declining to bid on the government requests. We maintained a mobilization agreement with the Department of Defense which would become active in the event of an all out war but that was it. We were required to review our plans every year to assure that we could meet the terms of our agreement. However, since the Jet Plant and Buildings 28 and 37 were now actively engaged in automotive production, alternate locations had to be developed.

Olds was fortunate to have a continuing expansion program underway during many of these years. Each of the new buildings would be partly allocated to war production if we had to again make guns. We called this our "guns and butter program" meaning we could also make cars in the various plans developed. We never planned to cease car production under any of the scenarios. On the pages that follow, are some of the plans which

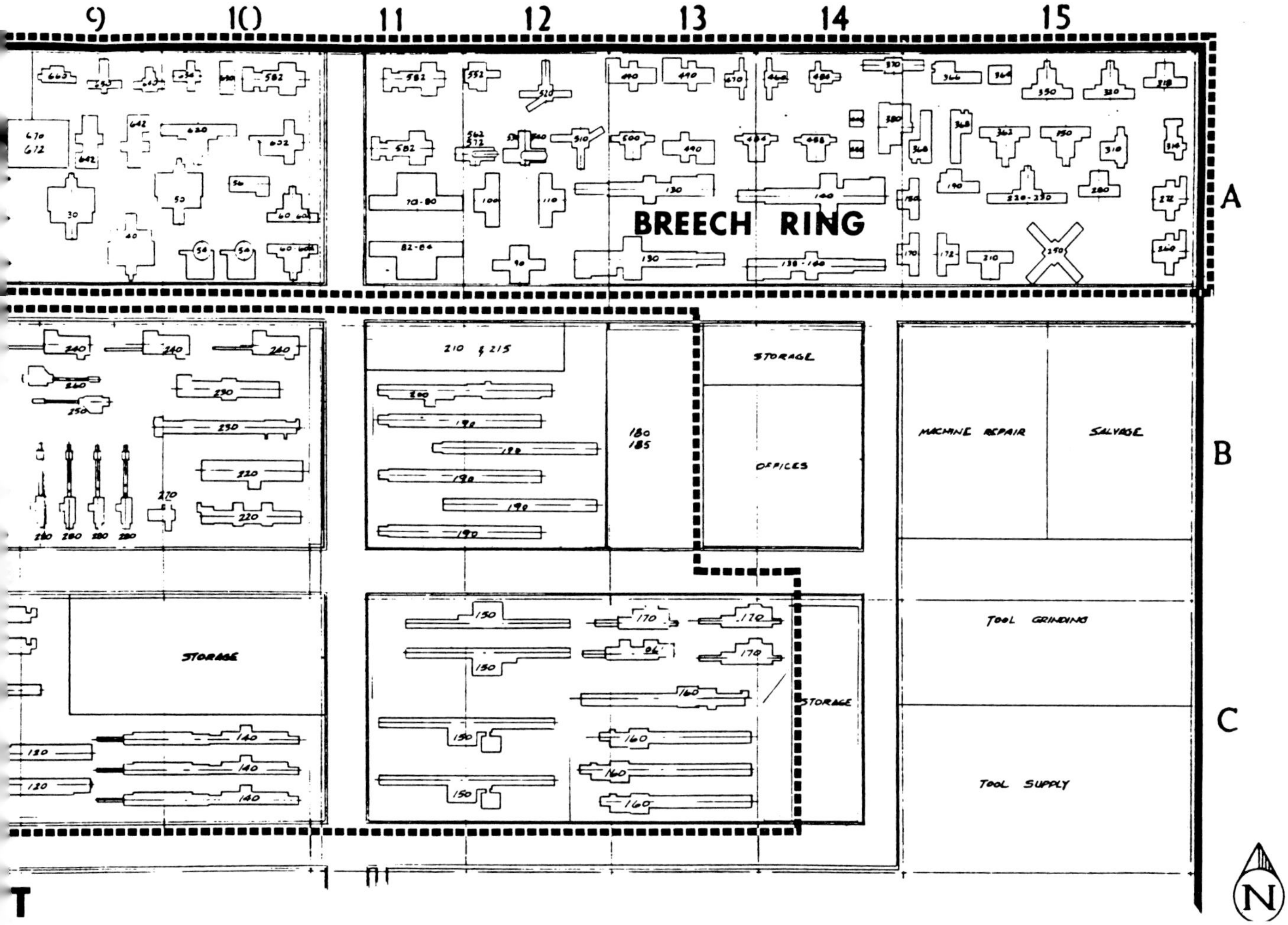

Later Activities

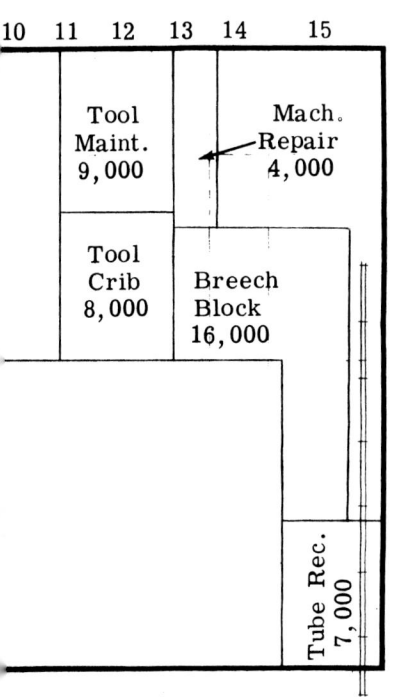

were created during this 15 year activity. The new Parts Warehouse (Plant 4) and Building 304-5 were two of the areas chosen as potential sites for cannon production.

Eventually, the types of rockets and cannon which we had produced became somewhat obsolete. We were continually being asked to quote other weapon systems which we had little or no experience making. The machinery which was stored to make the rockets and guns was also becoming obsolete. This equipment was stored in government warehouses, some as close as Pontiac. We also went to these locations to inspect the "warehouse package" to assure that it still was all there and capable of making the various parts we needed.

As time wore on, it became increasingly difficult to maintain our "guns and butter" approach. Car volumes were increasing rapidly and we needed all the space we had.

In the 1970s, Olds decided not to renew the mobilization agreement and since then has played no part in the production of war materiel. The 1966 and 1971 Bldg. 304 plans are shown here.

Later Activities

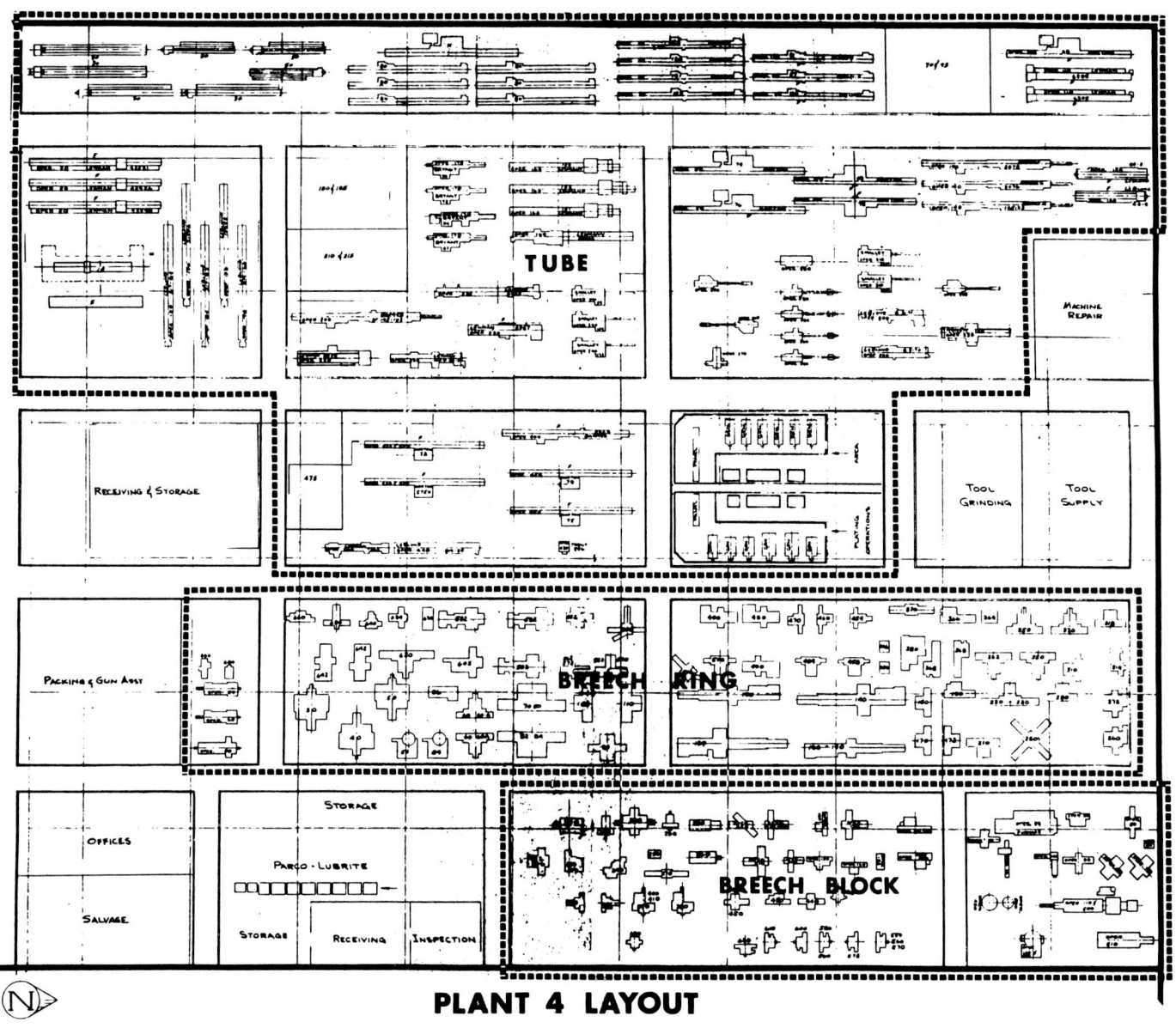

PLANT 4 LAYOUT

This page-In addition to using Bldg. 304, the Plant 4 buildings were set aside for potential production sites. The map above is for the north end of Bldg. 401. It is arranged for 90mm cannon production.

Opposite page-The 1969 Bldg. 304 plan for 90mm cannon production. After Bldg. 304 came into the picture, it became the main focus for our mobilization agreement production location.

Later Activities

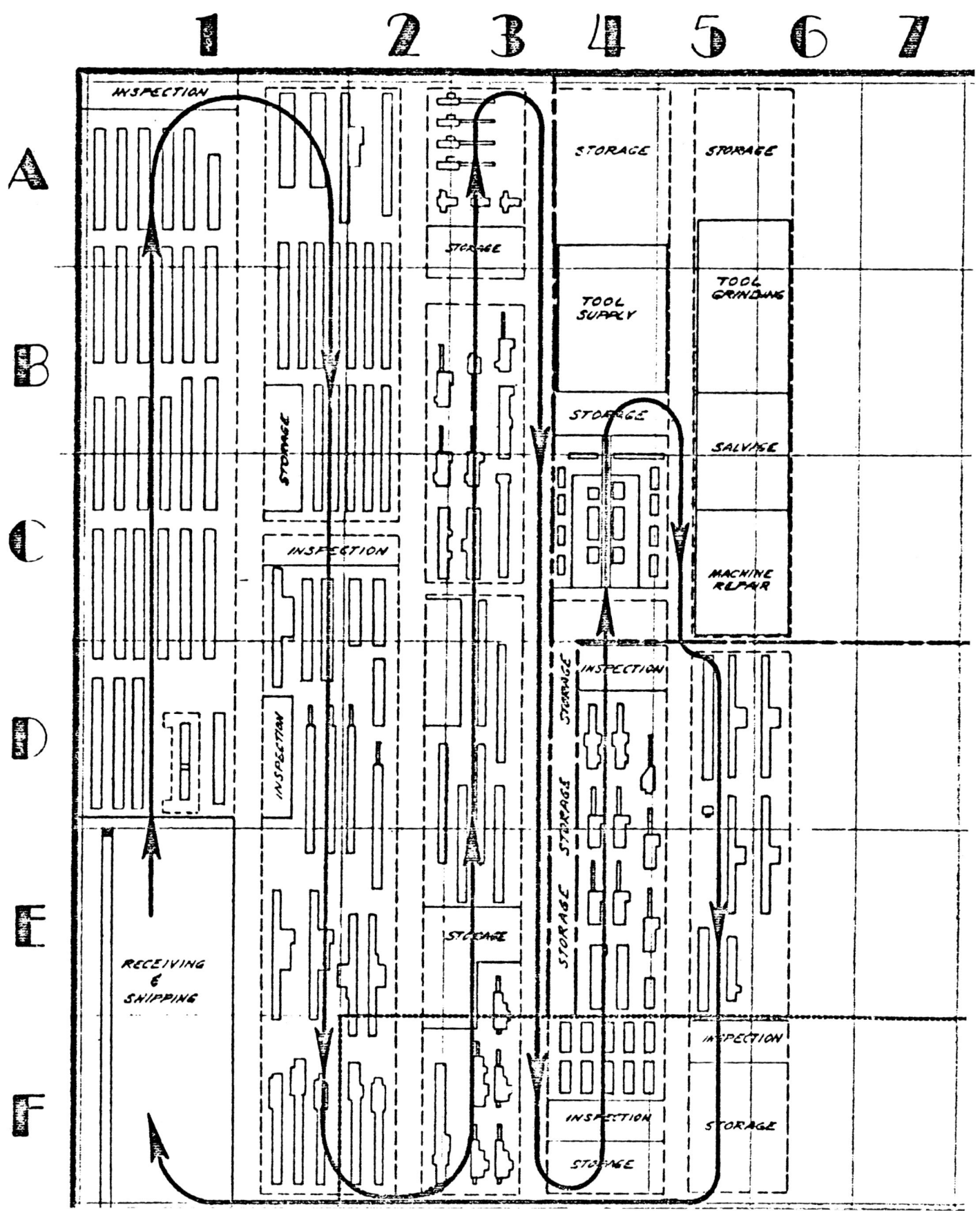

205

Appendix

World War I

Produced
> 2,100 mobile kitchen trailers for the aircraft service
> Contract Aug. 16, 1918, started manufacturing in Nov. 1918, completed in Jan. 1919

Contracted
> Liberty aircraft engines. Contract date Oct. 1918. Never started, war ended Nov. 11, 1918

Quoted but never put into production
> Trousers for the Army Oct. 5, 1918 date quoted
> Engine spares Nov. 14, 1918 date quoted

World War II Production

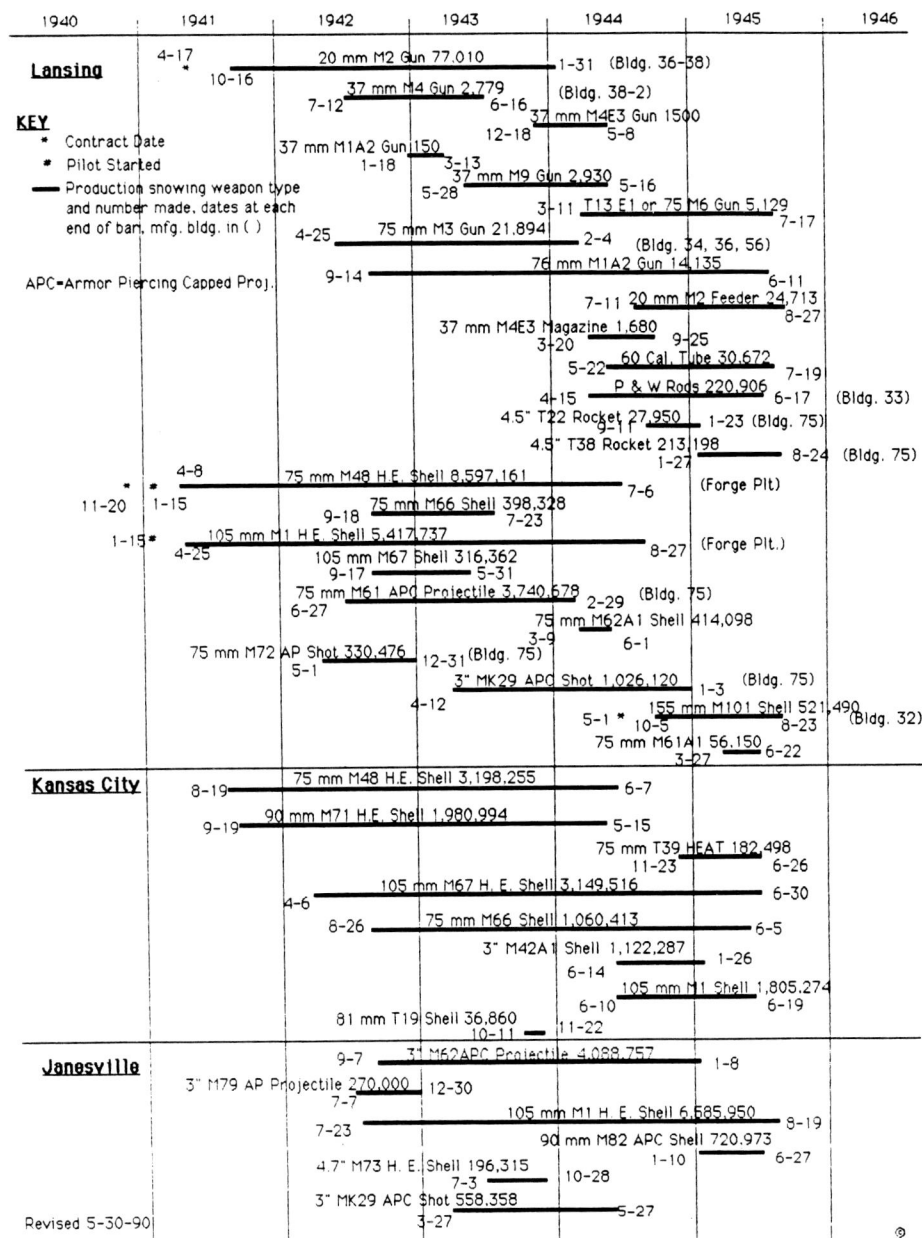

Appendix

Korean War

	1951	1952	1953	1954	1955	1956
Produced						
3.5" Rocket						
Motor metal parts	1,086,741	3,161,572	3,824,367	400,320		
Trap and spacer		3,161,572	3,824,367	400,320		
Head metal parts	488,620	1,874,480	1,032,900	2,509		
Practice head	684,647	1,896,743	2,108,735	10,950		
90mm T119 gun						
Gun assembly	453	3,704	1,274			
Tube	701	4,743	2,850			
Breech block	548	4,032	1,634			
Breech ring	454	3,854	957			
90mm T139						
Gun assembly				1,399	200	
Tube				1,685	1,162	
Breech block				1,594	132	
Breech ring				1,481	118	
90mm M41						
Gun assembly					991	485
Tube					1,687	854
Breech block					1,050	442
Breech ring					1,029	452
Jet engine rotating members J65 B1						
Turbine assembly		23	1,036	2,004	1,324	
Compressor assembly		15	1,012	2,259	1,313	
Compressor assembly for Wright			122		^--J65B7 engine	
30mm gun T121						
Gun assembly				7	28	

Quotes Requested-No bid
  Reworking 105mm M1 projectiles 1950
  Reworking 90mm M71 projectiles 1950
  90mm M41 1951, 1953, 10-25-55
  M2A4 mine 1952
  2.75" rocket 1952
  3.5" rocket T230 6-2-52
  Recoilless rifle 9-16-52
  90mm cannon M3A1 3-12-53
  Rocket parts Nat. Gypsum Co. 10-23-53
  Gun 20mm M6 chargers 10-23-53
  3.5" rocket live heads 10-12-54
  Rocket parts T205 12-8-54
  Rocket parts M28A2 8-3-55
  Rocket parts M28A2 8-12-55
  Rocket M35 7-5-56
  90mm gun bearing 7-16-57

Bids Rejected
  3.5" rocket T127E3 3-12-52
  76mm M42A1Shell 4-18-52
  60mm Mortar shell M302 4-18-52
  76mm gun M1A2 6-16-52

The Following Years

Mobilization Agreements, bid RFQ's and years

3.5" rocket	1960, 1965, 1972
76mm M32 gun	1969, 1970
90mm M41/M3A2 cannon	1962, 1969
90mm M36 cannon	1970
105mm M68 cannon	1962, 1971
152mm M81/XM162 cannon	1969
Camshaft M60 tank	1969
105mm projectile	1966
Station wagon conversion	1963
Windshield forging 152mm gun	1967

Index

Symbols

10,000th cannon   41
105mm shell   12, 48, 50
155mm M101 shell   46
155mm shell   50-55
20mm cannon   12-21, 132
20mm M2 cannon parts   14
3" M7 gun parts   59
3.5" bazooka rocket   180-189
30mm cannon   200-201
37mm cannon   22-29
37mm M1A2 cannon   22
37mm M4 cannon parts   22
37mm M9 cannon parts   24
4.5" T22 rocket   67
75mm cannon   13, 30-44, 131
75mm cannon parts   45
75mm M3 cannon parts   30
75mm M48 shell   46
75mm shell   12, 47, 48
76mm M1A2 cannon   30
90mm Cannon   190-199, 204

A

Abbott, Byron   155
Adams, Joseph   123
Advertising   80-95
Ahern, Geraldine   123
Ahler, Agatha   119
Ahler, Betty   119
American Broach   19
Amundson, Ruth   130
Auditorium   117
Automobile Topics   10
Auxiliary Military Police   136

B

Baker, W.   101
Barbour, Wilma   119
Barker, Don   119
Barlow, George   158
Barnhart, Leo   74
Barrel life   19
Basketball   119
Bauerle, Delos   157
Baumann, Otto   48
Bennett, Bernice   158
Bennett, William   114
Betts, William   74
Bigelow, Oral   54
Birney, Jim   191
Bissell, Warren   157
Blades, Charlie   123
Bldg. 20   8
Bldg. 21   7, 8, 10
Bldg. 32-75 plant layout   46
Bldg. 33   60
Bldg. 33/40 cafeterias   157
Bldg. 34   30
Bldg. 36   17, 20, 30, 41, 42
Bldg. 37   191
Bldg. 38   22
Bldg. 44   69, 123, 153, 167
Bldg. 56   30, 45
Bldg. 60   57, 125
Bldg. 60 Christmas   110
Bldg. 60 lobby   137, 153, 158
Bldg. 64   97
Bldg. 75   153
Bldgs. 36-38   153
Bldg. 201   70
Bldg. 202   70
Bldg. 203   70
Bldg. 204   70
Bldg. 304   203-4
Bldg. 401   204
Boch, Frank   119
Bond drive citation   105
Bond drives   102-109
Bowden, James   123, 139, 155
Brandel, C.   107
Brandel, A.   157
Breech ring   37, 191, 198
British War Orphans   117
Brooks, Marjorie   104
Brown, Donaldson   133
Buerge, Viola   52
Buick   8

Bullseye   101, 157
Bunce, William   157
Bureau of Aircraft Production   10
Burnham, Don   172, 180, 191, 194
Buy a Bomber   106

C

Cannoneer   108, 138
Carbide tools   59
Carter, Walter   157
Childs, Monty   200
Clean and finish   76
Cline, Willene   119
Cook, Robert J.   5
Cook, Theodore   139
Cornell, Maynard   200
Courtright, Clarence   119
Crawford, Sam   158
Culp, Estol   157
Cushman, Edith   114

D

Dakin, C. B.   76, 160
Deschow, Fred   119
Display   41, 56-57, 110, 151
Division St. gate   136
Dobbs, J. J.   99
Downey, Tom   180, 191, 194
Dykhoff, Albert   107
Dykstra, John   34, 132-133

E

E Award   48, 120-123
E flag   123, 153
Earley, Helen   4, 158
Earley, William   157
Eckhart, Roland   60
Economy Truck   10-11
Edwards, Jim   191
Eisenhower, General Dwight   145, 147
Employment office   125
Engine spares   10
Entertainment   110-119
Erie steam hammer   76

F

Fire-power   12
Firewagon   158
Fish, Clarence   158
Fong, Dr. H. D.   137
Force, Phyllis   119
Forge Plant   12, 70-71
Forge Plant construction   162-165
Forge Plant flag pole   160-161
Forging   47, 72-79
Fork rods   131
Fort Custer band   123
Fouke, Phillip Bond, III   135
Freeman, John   74
Fuller, Dewey   64
Fuller, Helen   117

G

Gardner, Helen   131
Gillespie, Brig. Gen. A. G.   114, 121, 123
Glass, Charles   200
GM Forge Plant #1   46, 70
GM Forge Plant #2   46
GM Girls club   117
GM Victory Review   112
Gothro, Ken   119
Granstrom, John   63
Griffin, R.   157
Griffin, R. E.   36
Gun school   96-101, 158
Gun test   68-69, 122, 152, 167
Gun test 37mm   69
Guns and butter program   202

H

Hale, Howard   200
Hansen, Arnold   192
Harvey, Arnold   119
Hasbany, Fred   107
Havens, C.   139
Hayes, Helen   102
Hemmer, Bettye   157
Henry, Jack   119
Hess, Rosa   114
Hidlay, H.   101
Hookway, Honoura   114

Hopkins, R.   119
Hopkins, Revell   157
Hoskins, Chester   133
Howell, Charles   79

I

Ingham County War Fund Drive   102

J

Janesville   46
Janesville E flag   123
JC's   157
Jet Plant   169-179
Johnson, Harry   52

K

Kansas City   46
Keep 'em Firing   13, 138
Keep 'em Rolling   154
Kemp, Bill   119
kitchen trailers   6
Konen, Walter   60
Krathwohl, Charles   55

L

Laverty, Linda   158
Laverty, Sharon   158
Leamy, Dorothy   105
Liberty Aircraft Engine   7-10
Lindner, Ed   36
Linn, Emil   106
Long, James   119

M

M4 tank   30, 38
MacArthur, General Douglas   200
MacArthur Visit   200
Mahoney, Bill   114
McCree, Bessie   114
McCumby, George   74
McElmurry, Daryl   119
McHenry, H. S.   98
McKane, Kenneth   157
McLeod, Roy   119
McRae, Del   172, 179, 192
McWilliams, Alva   106
Metzel, Harold   194
Michigan Theater   112, 125
Miller, Lila   52
Mobilization agreement   202
Monoski, Ed   101
Moon, Harold   105
Morton, Laura   48
Mullett, Hazel   119
Murphy, F.   157
Myers, R.   157

N

Nader, George   139
Newhouse, Frank   119
Newman, Glenn   74
Niblick, Ray   158
Niblick, Roy   158
Nisbet, Bob   119
Northway V-8 engine   7
Norton, Erma   114

O

Olds, Ransom   134-135
Open house   79, 119

P

Pacemaker   7, 8
Padgett, Lyle   119, 157
Palmer, Ken   119
Parades   7
Parking lot 8   137
Parts Warehouse   203
Patterson, Robert   145
Pere Marquette   10
Perkins, Rome   107
Pierce, John   76
Pine Street gate   167
Plant 1   12, 13
Plant 1 plant layout   12
Plant 2   13, 46, 70-71
Plant 2 plant layout   12

Plant 3   202-203, 205
Plant 4   202-204
Plant Security   136
Pohl, Harold   139
Pollock, Dick   114
Powers, Willard   119
Pratt and Whitney   19
Pratt and Whitney blade turners   172
Pratt and Whitney rods   60-63
Purchis, Homer   136

Q

Quarter Century Club   114
Quartermaster Corps   10
Quinton, Col. A. B. Jr.   121

R

Ralston, David E.   35
Receiving inspection   59
Red Cross   158
Riebow, L.   179
Rifling   18
Roberts, R.   139
Rockets   66-67
Roll of Honor   153
Rolls Royce Merlin cranks   64-65
Ryder, Barbara   119

S

Safety glasses   125
Safety store   153, 158
Saier, Felicitas   159
Sanders, Fred   107
Schuon, Earl   105
Schwab, Floyd   136
Scott, Bob   179
Scrap drives   154, 155
Sergeant, H.   59
Sermak, A.   63
Seymour, Fred   114
Sharp, Burk   114
Shaw, Ruth   131
Shell display   57
Sherman, Leroy   157
Shot blasting   130
Signage   138-153
Skinner, Beverly   119
Skinner, Sherrod   105, 114, 123, 132, 155, 180, 194
Sloan, Alfred   132-135
Small press area   59
Snood   128
Somervell, General   155
Standish, D.   155
State Police firing range   136, 137
Szpara, W.   171

T

Taylor, Dave   79
Taylor, Leo   74
Telegrams   145
Tires   154
Trousers   10
Tycocki, Ted   119

V

"V" for victory   57, 104
Valek, Frank   74
VanWagoner, Gov. Murrary   121
Ver Merris, Elmer   157
Victory gardens   117

W

Waite, Leslis   74
Walker, Rocky   119
Walkinshaw, Jim   4
Washington display   151
Waters, Jack   119
Weber, Stanley   107
Westman, A.   101
Whitney Olds   154
Wilcox, Hazen   139
Wiles, John   158
Wilkins, Jeanette   159
Wilson, Charles   132, 133, 180, 194, 200
Wilson, Harold   139
Wings   112, 124-125
WJIM radio   102, 151
Wolfram, Jack   172, 180, 191, 194
Women in the Workplace   124-132
Wright J-65 jet engine   169
WWII end   165, 167